WORDS THAT SET US FREE

★ ★ ★

A Documentary History & Chronology
of America's Struggle for Equal Justice & Civil Rights

The Editors of the World Almanac

WORLD ALMANAC
AN IMPRINT OF PHAROS BOOKS · A SCRIPPS HOWARD COMPANY
NEW YORK

> *Dedicated to the Memory of Christopher Fuhrman*

First published in 1992.

Library of Congress Cataloging-in-Publication Data
Words that set us free : a documentary history and chronology of America's struggle for equal justice and civil rights / by the editors of the World almanac.
p. cm.
ISBN 0-88687-680-X
1. Civil rights—United States—History—Sources. I. World almanac.
JC599.U5W667 1992
323′.0973—dc20   92-1192   CIP

Printed in the United States of America

Cover design: Sara Stemen
Interior design: Janet Tingey

Pharos Books
A Scripps Howard Company
200 Park Avenue
New York, NY 10166

10 9 8 7 6 5 4 3 2 1

Pharos Books are available at special discounts on bulk purchases for sales promotions, premiums, fundraising or educational use. For details, contact the Special Sales Department, Pharos Books, 200 Park Avenue, New York, NY 10166

FOREWORD

The recent bicentennial celebrations of the Constitution and of the Bill of Rights have underscored the longevity of America's experiment in democracy and individual freedom. Yet few of these observations have explored the fact that many of the liberties enshrined in these documents were a long time in coming for the vast majority of Americans. When the Constitution was ratified, millions of black Americans were held in slavery, considered mere property to be sold at the discretion of their owners. American women had no civil or economic rights, and many white males were denied suffrage for religious or economic reasons.

Words That Set Us Free is a brief and accessible history of the courageous men and women who spoke out against injustice and challenged the prevailing status quo. It must be remembered that when Frederick Douglass fought against slavery, he was up against an institution sanctioned by the Constitution and considered perfectly acceptable by the majority of Americans. When Susan B. Anthony railed against the subservience of women, she was questioning a role that many considered preordained by God. Almost every crusader cited or quoted in this book risked their social standing, their freedom and their very lives to challenge an unjust social order.

While *Words That Set Us Free* should be read as inspirational history, it is also a cautionary tale. It shows how quickly progress has been undone by forces of reaction and expedience. It is sobering to note how quickly the great Fourteenth Amendment was rendered impotent by courts unwilling to question state-sponsored racism. Nor did it take very long for "Jim Crow" to become the law of the land once the federal government walked away from Reconstruction.

Today's readers should keep in mind that many of the laws and reforms that have emerged from our most recent struggles for civil rights for black Americans, women and *all* Americans have been in place for less than a single generation. If history is any guide, there is no guarantee that these reforms will not be diluted or swept away. If there is a lesson to be learned from *Words That Set Us Free*, it is that even our most fundamental laws can be reduced to empty words if not vigilantly defended by citizens of conscience.

1775

April 14: The first Abolitionist society, the Society for the Relief of Free Negroes Unlawfully Held in Bondage, is founded by Benjamin Franklin and Benjamin Rush.

August: The first article proposing women's rights is published in Tom Paine's *Pennsylvania Magazine*.

1776

Thomas Jefferson proposes African resettlement of slaves.

March 31: Abigail Adams writes to her husband John, a member of the Continental Congress and future president, reminding him that any fight against British tyranny must include women's rights.

ABIGAIL ADAMS, IN A LETTER TO JOHN ADAMS

I long to hear that you have declared an independancy—and by the way in the new Code of Laws which I suppose it will be necessary for you to make I desire you would Remember the Ladies, and be more generous and favour-

able to them than your ancestors. Do not put such unlimited power into the hands of the Husbands. Remember all Men would be tyrants if they could. If perticuliar care and attention is not paid to the Ladies we are determined to foment a Rebelion, and will not hold ourselves bound by any Laws in which we have no voice, or Representation.

July 2: Colony of New Jersey grants women's suffrage. Law will remain in effect until 1807.

July 4: The Declaration of Independence is signed in Philadelphia.

The Declaration of Independence

When in the Course of human Events, it become necessary for one People to dissolve the Political Bands which have connected them with another, and to assume among the Powers of the Earth, the separate and equal Station to which the Laws of Nature and of Nature's God entitle them, a decent Respect to the Opinions of Mankind requires that they should declare the causes which impel them to the Separation.

We hold these Truths to be self-evident, that all Men are created equal, that they are endowed by their Creator with certain unalienable Rights, that among these are Life, Liberty, and the Pursuit of Happiness—That to secure these Rights, Governments are instituted among

Men, deriving their just Powers from the Consent of the Governed, that whenever any Form of Government becomes destructive of these Ends, it is the Right of the People to alter or to abolish it, and to institute new Government, laying its Foundation on such Principles, and organizing its Powers in such Form, as to them shall seem most likely to effect their Safety and Happiness. Prudence, indeed, will dictate that Governments long established should not be changed for light and transient Causes; and accordingly all Experience hath shewn, that Mankind are more disposed to suffer, while Evils are sufferable, than to right themselves by abolishing the Forms to which they are accustomed. But when a long Train of Abuses and Usurpations, pursuing invariably the same Object, evinces a Design to reduce them under absolute Despotism, it is their Right, it is their Duty, to throw off such Government, and to provide new Guards for their future Security. Such has been the patient Sufferance of these Colonies; and such is now the Necessity which constrains them to alter their former Systems of Government. The History of the present King of Great-Britain is a History of repeated Injuries and Usurpations, all having in direct Object the Establishment of an absolute Tyranny over these States. To prove this, let Facts be submitted to a candid World.

He has refused his Assent to Laws, the most wholesome and necessary for the public Good.

He has forbidden his Governors to pass Laws of immediate and pressing Importance, unless suspended in their

Operation till his Assent should be obtained; and when so suspended, he has utterly neglected to attend to them.

He has refused to pass other Laws for the Accommodation of large Districts of People, unless those People would relinquish the Right of Representation in the Legislature, a Right inestimable to them, and formidable to Tyrants only.

He has called together Legislative Bodies at Places unusual, uncomfortable, and distant from the Depository of their Public Records, for the sole Purpose of fatiguing them into Compliance with his Measures.

He has dissolved Representative Houses repeatedly, for opposing with manly Firmness his Invasions on the Rights of the People.

He has refused for a long Time, after such Dissolutions, to cause others to be elected; whereby the Legislative Powers, incapable of Annihilation, have returned to the People at large for their exercise; the State remaining in the mean time exposed to all the Dangers of Invasion from without, and Convulsions within.

He has endeavoured to prevent the Population of these States; for that Purpose obstructing the Laws for Naturalization of Foreigners; refusing to pass others to encourage their Migrations hither, and raising the Conditions of new Appropriations of Lands.

He has obstructed the Administration of Justice, by refusing his Assent to Laws for establishing Judiciary Powers.

He has made Judges dependent on his Will alone, for the Tenure of their Offices, and the Amount and payment of their Salaries.

He has erected a Multitude of new Offices, and sent hither Swarms of Officers to harrass our People, and eat out their Substance.

He has kept among us, in Times of Peace, Standing Armies, without the consent of our Legislatures.

He has affected to render the Military independent of, and superior to the Civil Power.

He has combined with others to subject us to a Jurisdiction foreign to our Constitution, and unacknowledged by our Laws; giving his Assent to their Acts of pretended Legislation:

For quartering large Bodies of Armed Troops among us:

For protecting them, by a mock Trial, from Punishment for any Murders which they should commit on the Inhabitants of these States:

For cutting off our Trade with all Parts of the World:

For imposing Taxes on us without our Consent:

For depriving us, in many Cases, of the Benefits of Trial by Jury:

For transporting us beyond Seas to be tried for pretended Offences:

For abolishing the free System of English Laws in a neighbouring Province, establishing therein an arbitrary Government, and enlarging its Boundaries, so as to render it at once an Example and fit Instrument for introducing the same absolute Rule into these Colonies:

For taking away our Charters, abolishing our most valuable Laws, and altering fundamentally the Forms of our Governments:

For suspending our own Legislatures, and declaring themselves invested with Power to legislate for us in all Cases whatsoever.

He has abdicated Government here, by declaring us out of his Protection and waging War against us.

He has plundered our Seas, ravaged our Coasts, burnt our towns, and destroyed the Lives of our People.

He is, at this Time, transporting large Armies of foreign Mercenaries to compleat the works of Death, Desolation, and Tyranny, already begun with circumstances of Cruelty and Perfidy, scarcely paralleled in the most barbarous Ages, and totally unworthy the Head of a civilized Nation.

He has constrained our fellow Citizens taken Captive on the high Seas to bear Arms against their Country, to become the Executioners of their Friends and Brethren, or to fall themselves by their Hands.

He has excited domestic Insurrections amongst us, and has endeavoured to bring on the Inhabitants of our Frontiers, the merciless Indian Savages, whose known Rule of Warfare, is an undistinguished Destruction, of all Ages, Sexes and Conditions.

In every stage of these Oppressions we have Petitioned for Redress in the most humble Terms: Our repeated Petitions have been answered only by repeated Injury. A Prince, whose Character is thus marked by every act which may define a Tyrant, is unfit to be the Ruler of a free People.

Nor have we been wanting in Attentions to our British Brethren. We have warned them from Time to Time of Attempts by their Legislature to extend an unwarrantable Jurisdiction over us. We have reminded them of the Circumstances of our Emigration and Settlement here. We have appealed to their native Justice and Magnanimity, and we have conjured them by the Ties of our common Kindred to disavow these Usurpations, which, would inevitably interrupt our Connections and Correspondence. They too have been deaf to the Voice of Justice and of Consanguinity. We must, therefore, acquiesce in the Necessity, which denounces our Separation, and hold them, as we hold the rest of Mankind, Enemies in War, in Peace, Friends.

We, therefore, the Representatives of the UNITED STATES OF AMERICA, in General Congress, Assembled, appealing to the Supreme Judge of the World for the Rectitude of our Intentions, do, in the Name, and by Authority of the good People of these Colonies, solemnly Publish and Declare, That these United Colonies are, and of Right ought to be, Free and Independent States; that they are absolved from all Allegiance to the British Crown, and that all political Connection between them and the State of Great-Britain, is and ought to be totally dissolved; and that as Free and Independent States, they have full Power to levy War, conclude Peace, contract Alliances, establish Commerce, and to do all other Acts

*and Things which Independent States may of right do.
And for the support of this declaration, with a firm Reli-
ance on the Protection of divine Providence, we mutually
pledge to each other our lives, our Fortunes, and our
sacred Honor.*

A passage denouncing King George's encouragement of
the slave trade is deleted from the Declaration. It is considered too offensive to Southern slaveholders and New
England merchants who profit from slave trafficing.

An Anti-Slavery Passage Deleted from the Declaration of Independence

*He has waged cruel war against human nature itself,
violating its most sacred rights of life and liberty in the
persons of a distant people who never offended him, capti-
vating and carrying them into slavery in another hemi-
sphere, or to incur miserable death in their transportation
thither. This piratical warfare, the opprobrium of infidel
powers, is the warfare of the Christian king of Great
Britain. Determined to keep open a market where MEN
should be bought and sold, he has prostituted his negative
for suppressing every legislative attempt to prohibit or to
restrain this execrable commerce; and that this assem-
blage of horrors might want no fact of distinguished die,
he is now exciting these very people to rise in arms among
us, and to purchase that liberty of which he deprived
them, by murdering the people upon whom he also ob-
truded them; thus paying off former crimes committed*

against the liberties of one people, with crimes which he urges them to commit against the lives of another.

1780

Pennsylvania is the first state to abolish slavery.

1786

January 16: Virginia legislature adopts the Ordinance of Religious Freedom, written by Thomas Jefferson. A model for the First Amendment, this law guarantees that no man can be forced to observe or support any particular religion or be discriminated against because of his beliefs.

1787

December 7: Delaware is the first state to ratify the U.S. Constitution. To ensure support of slaveholding states, the document bars any prohibition or limitation of slave importation until at least 1808. It also includes the "three-fifths rule": in any census, five slaves count as three free whites. Thus slavery is incorporated, yet never mentioned, in the Constitution. As Abraham Lincoln will state two generations later, *The thing [slavery] is hid away in the Constitution, just as an afflicted man hides away a wen or cancer which he dares not cut out at once, lest he bleed to death.*

*   *   *

July 13: The Northwest Ordinance is passed by Continental Congress. It establishes the Northwest Territories and bans slavery within the territories.

1790

The first national census notes that only 9% of 757,000 black Americans are free.

February 11: First emancipation petition is submitted to Congress by the Society of Friends (Quakers).

1791

Even though thousands of blacks fought in the Revolutionary War, Congress excludes blacks and Native Americans from service in the peacetime militia.

January 5: Free blacks in South Carolina petition the state legislature to end prohibition of black-initiated lawsuits. The protest is rejected.

June 13: Slaves revolt in the Spanish territory of Louisiana. 23 slaves are hanged.

December 15: The Bill of Rights goes into effect.

THE ORIGINAL AMENDMENTS: THE BILL OF RIGHTS

Amendment 1.
[Religious establishment prohibited. Freedom of speech, of the press, and right to petition.]

Congress shall make no law respecting an establishment of religion, or prohibiting the free exercise thereof; or abridging the freedom of speech, or of the press; or the right of the people peaceably to assemble, and to petition the Government for a redress of grievances.

Amendment II.
[Right to keep and bear arms.]

A well-regulated militia, being necessary to the security of a free State, the right of the people to keep and bear arms, shall not be infringed.

Amendment III.
[Conditions for quarters for soldiers.]

No soldier shall, in time of peace be quartered in any house, without the consent of the owner, nor in time of war, but in a manner to be prescribed by law.

Amendment IV.
[Right of search and seizure regulated.]

The right of the people to be secure in their persons, houses, papers, and effects, against unreasonable searches

*and seizures, shall not be violated, and no warrants shall
issue, but upon probable cause, supported by oath or affirmation, and particularly describing the place to be
searched, and the persons or things to be seized.*

Amendment V.
*[Provisions concerning prosecution. Trial and
punishment—private property not to be taken for
public use without compensation.]*

*No person shall be held to answer for a capital, or
otherwise infamous crime, unless on a presentment or
indictment of a Grand Jury, except in cases arising in the
land or naval forces, or in the militia, when in actual
service in time of war or public danger; nor shall any
person be subject for the same offense to be twice put in
jeopardy of life or limb; nor shall be compelled in any
criminal case to be a witness against himself, nor be deprived of life, liberty, or property, without due process of
law; nor shall private property be taken for public use
without just compensation.*

Amendment VI.
[Right to speedy trial, witnesses, etc.]

*In all criminal prosecutions, the accused shall enjoy the
right to a speedy and public trial, by an impartial jury of
the State and district wherein the crime shall have been
committed, which district shall have been previously as-*

certained by law, and to be informed of the nature and cause of the accusation; to be confronted with the witnesses against him; to have compulsory process for obtaining witnesses in his favor, and to have the assistance of counsel for his defense.

Amendment VII.
[Right of trial by jury.]

In suits at common law, where the value in controversy shall exceed twenty dollars, the right of trial by jury shall be preserved, and no fact tried by a jury shall be otherwise reexamined in any court of the United States, than according to the rules of the common law.

Amendment VIII.
[Excessive bail or fines and cruel punishment prohibited.]

Excessive bail shall not be required, nor excessive fines imposed, nor cruel and unusual punishments inflicted.

Amendment IX.
[Rule of construction of Constitution.]

The enumeration in the Constitution, of certain rights, shall not be construed to deny or disparage others retained by the people.

Amendment X.
[Rights of States under Constitution.]

The powers not delegated to the United States by the Constitution, nor prohibited by it to the States, are reserved to the States respectively, or to the people.

April: At Kentucky's constitutional convention, Presbyterian clergyman Daniel Rice makes an unsuccessful attempt to ban slavery from the state.

George Mason makes an unsuccessful attempt to ban slavery from Virginia, calling it "a disgrace to mankind."

Denmark is the first nation to abolish its slave trade.

Inspired by the principles of the American Revolution, British writer Mary Wollstonecraft writes *A Vindication of the Rights of Woman.*

1793

Implementing Article IV, Section 2, of the new Constitution, Congress passes the Fugitive Slave Act, making it a crime to harbor escaped slaves or prevent their arrest.

Virginia passes a law forbidding entry of free blacks into the state.

1796

St. George Tucker, law professor at the College of William and Mary, argues that slavery is inconsistent with the high moral purpose of the Bill of Rights.

June 1: Tennessee is admitted to the Union as a slave state.

1797

Congress refuses to accept the first recorded anti-slavery petition, which questions the legality of a North Carolina law requiring that all freed slaves be returned to the state as slaves.

1798

The U.S. Navy and Marines bar black enlistment.

1799

March 29: The New York legislature passes a law allowing gradual emancipation of slaves.

1800

January 2: Free blacks from Philadelphia petition Congress, asking for an end to the institution of slavery, the slave trade, and the Fugitive Slave Act. Congress ignores them.

The Virginia State Assembly passes a nonbinding resolution proposing African resettlement of slaves.

Congress votes 85-1 to reject a petition proposing a gradual end to slavery.

1804

Ohio becomes the first of several Northern states to enact "black laws" restricting the rights and movement of black Americans.

New Jersey abolishes slavery.

1807

March 2: Congress bans slave importation, effective January 1, 1808.

1808

The Louisiana court, in *Adelle v. Beauregard*, rules that black Americans are free unless proven otherwise.

1811

Delaware forbids entry of free blacks.

1816

Louisiana law forbids slaves from testifying against whites or free blacks, except in trials concerning slave uprisings.

December 28: A Presbyterian minister founds American Colonialization Society, calling for black resettlement of Africa.

Connecticut extends suffrage to all white male adults, eliminating property qualifications. Black voters are disenfranchised.

1819

James Madison argues for the end of slavery. He also proposes that blacks be allotted homelands in the West to ensure separation of the races.

March 2: Congress passes the first immigration law, regulating ships and establishing accurate registry of new arrivals.

March 3: As illegal slave importation continues, Congress passes a law calling for a $50 reward per slave for information leading to the arrest of smugglers.

1820

February 6: First organized emigration to Africa; 86 freed slaves sail to Sierra Leone on the *Mayflower of Liberia*.

March 3: Congress passes the Missouri Compromise, admitting Maine as a free state and Missouri as a slave state, and banning slavery in the Louisiana Territory south of Missouri's border.

May 15: Congress declares slave smuggling to be act of piracy and establishes the death penalty for illegal importers.

July 19: Missouri drafts a state constitution barring entry of free blacks and mulattoes.

1821

Benjamin Lundy establishes his Abolitionist journal, *The Genius of Universal Emancipation*.

The West African nation of Liberia is founded by the American Colonialization Society.

1822

May 30: Freed slave Denmark Vesey leads an uprising in an attempt to seize control of Charleston, South Carolina. Vesey and 34 others are executed.

1825

Eight Northern state legislatures propose emancipation of all slaves at federal expense.

1826

Pennsylvania nullifies the Fugitive Slave Act of 1793.

In his last will and testament, Thomas Jefferson frees only five of his many slaves, leaving the rest to his heirs.

1827

March 16: *Freedom's Journal,* the first black newspaper in America, begins publication in New York City.

1828

William Lloyd Garrison, editor of the *National Philanthropist,* begins his attacks on slavery.

1829

Publication of the militant anti-slavery pamphlet *"An Appeal to the Colored Citizens of the World"* by David Walker, a free black, causes an uproar among slaveholders.

1831

January 1: Publication of the first issue of William Lloyd Garrison's *The Liberator*, the leading Abolitionist journal. In his prospectus, Garrison marks a change in tone from earlier calls for gradual emancipation. In *The Liberator*, he calls for an immediate end to an immoral institution.

FROM WILLIAM LLOYD GARRISON'S *The Liberator*

Assenting to the "self-evident truth" maintained in the American Declaration of Independence, "that all men are created equal and endowed by their Creator with certain inalienable rights—among which are life, liberty and the pursuit of happiness," I shall strenuously contend for the immediate enfranchisement of our slave population. In Park-street Church, on the Fourth of July, 1829, in an address on slavery, I unreflectingly assented to the popular but pernicious doctrine of gradual abolition. I seize this opportunity to make a full and unequivocal recantation, and thus publicly to ask pardon of my God, of my country, and of my brethren the poor slaves, for having uttered a sentiment so full of timidity, injustice and absurdity. A similar recantation, from my pen, was published in the Genius of Universal Emancipation *at Baltimore, in September, 1829. My conscience is now satisfied.*

I am aware that many object to the severity of my language; but is there not cause for severity? I will be as harsh as truth, and as uncompromising as justice. On this subject, I do not wish to think, or speak, or write, with moderation. No! no! Tell a man whose house is on fire, to give a moderate alarm; tell him to moderately rescue his wife from the hands of the ravisher; tell the mother to gradually extricate her babe from the fire into which it has fallen;—but urge me not to use moderation in a cause like the present. I am in earnest—I will not equivocate—I will not excuse—I will not retreat a single inch—AND I WILL BE HEARD. The apathy of the people is enough to make every statue leap from its pedestal, and to hasten the resurrection of the dead.

It is pretended, that I am retarding the cause of emancipation, by the coarseness of my invective, and the precipitancy of my measures. The charge is not true. On this question my influence,—humble as it is,—is felt at this moment to a considerable extent, and shall be felt in coming years—not perniciously, but beneficially—not as a curse, but as a blessing; and posterity will bear testimony that I was right. I desire to thank God, that he enables me to disregard "the fear of man which bringeth a snare," and to speak his truth in its simplicity and power. . . .

August 21–22: Black preacher Nat Turner leads an insurrection in Southampton County, Virginia. More than 50 whites and 100 slaves are killed. Turner is captured October 30 and hanged November 11. Fearful of more uprisings, Southern states censor Abolitionist publications.

1832

January 6: The New England Anti-Slavery Society is founded at the African Baptist Church in Boston.

January 21: The Virginia State Assembly debates the abolition of slavery. Thomas Jefferson Randolf presents his grandfather's plan for gradual emancipation.

1833

December 4: The American Anti-Slavery Society is founded in Philadelphia, with Lucretia Mott named president.

1834

Oberlin College is founded, the first American college to admit women.

Slavery is abolished in the British Empire.

South Carolina enacts a law outlawing education of slaves or freed blacks.

July 4–12: Anti-Abolitionist riots break out in New York City.

1835

Theodore Dwight Weld trains anti-slavery agents known as "The Seventy" to propagandize in rural Northern and border states.

William Ellery Channing publishes "Slavery," an Abolitionist tract.

Publication of Lydia Maria Child's *History of the Conditions of Women, in Various Ages and Nations.*

Georgia passes a law calling for the death penalty for those publishing material that might incite slave rebellions.

July 6: A pro-slavery mob in Charleston, South Carolina, burns Abolitionist literature impounded at the local post office.

October 21: Angered by anti-slavery speeches, including the phrase, "all men are created equal," a Boston mob attacks editor William Lloyd Garrison.

1836

January: Publication of the anti-slavery newspaper *Philanthropist* by James Birney.

Ernestine L. Rose submits a feminist petition to the New York State legislature requesting that married women retain the right to hold property in their own name.

The Massachusetts Supreme Court rules that any slaves brought across the state's border are free men.

January 11: Abolitionists petition Congress to end slavery in the District of Columbia.

March 17: Texas adopts a constitution legalizing slavery.

May 25: Flooded with anti-slavery petitions, the House of Representatives enacts a "gag rule" ending debate on the subject. The rule is renewed until 1844.

June 15: Arkansas is admitted to the Union as a slave state.

1837

Canada extends suffrage to black citizens.

February 6: U.S. House of Representatives passes a bill denying slaves the right of petition, a right guaranteed to U.S. citizens in the Constitution.

November 7: Abolitionist Elijah P. Lovejoy is killed by a mob in Alton, Illinois.

Raised among South Carolina's slave-holding aristocracy, Sarah and Angelina Grimké wage a zealous battle against the evils of slavery. Yet their public campaign is often startling to male fellow Abolitionists, who feel that women have no place in public debate.

ANGELINA GRIMKÉ ON A WOMAN'S PLACE IN GOVERNMENT

Now I believe it is a woman's right to have a voice in all the laws and regulations by which she is to be governed, whether in Church or State: and that the present arrangements of society, on these points, are a violation of human rights, a rank usurpation of power, a violent seizure and confiscation of what is sacredly and inalienably hers. . . . If Ecclesiastical and Civil governments are ordained of God, then I contend that woman has just as much right to sit in solemn counsel in conventions, conferences, associations and general assemblies, as man—just as much right to sit upon the throne of England or in the Presidential chair of the United States.

1838

Mirror of Liberty, the first black American periodical, is published in New York by David Ruggles, a black Abolitionist.

February: Angelina Grimké presents an anti-slavery petition signed by 20,000 women to the Massachusetts legislature. Her address is the first time a woman speaks before a legislative body.

From Angelina Grimké's Address to the Massachusett's Legislature

These petitions relate to the great and solemn subject of slavery. . . . And because it is a political subject, it has often tauntingly been said, that women had nothing to do with it. Are we aliens, because we are women? Are we bereft of citizenship because we are mothers, wives and daughters of a mighty people? Have women no country—no interests staked in public weal—no liabilities in common peril—no partnership in a nation's guilt and shame . . . ?

I hold, Mr. Chairman, that the American women have to do with this subject, not only because it is moral and religious, but because it is political, inasmuch as we are citizens of this republic and as such our honor, happiness and well-being are bound up in its politics, government and laws.

February 14: Defying the "gag rule," Massachusetts legislator and former President John Quincy Adams introduces 350 anti-slavery petitions in the House of Representatives.

May 17: Angered by Abolitionist meetings, a mob sets fire to Philadelphia's Pennsylvania Hall.

* * *

December 3: Representative Joshua Giddings (Whig—Ohio) is the first Abolitionist to enter Congress.

1839

U.S. State Department declines to issue passports for American blacks, citing noncitizenship.

Publication of *American Slavery As It Is*, by Abolitionist Theodore Dwight Weld.

Africans bound for slavery on the Spanish slave ship *Amistad* mutiny and the ship is brought into harbor in Montauk, New York. African leader Cinque and followers are defended before the U.S. Supreme Court by former President John Quincy Adams, and awarded their freedom.

February 7: In an attack on Abolitionists, Kentucky Senator Henry Clay warns that anti-slavery agitation will result in civil war.

November 13: The anti-slavery Liberty party holds a national convention and nominates James G. Birney for president.

1840

Pope Gregory XVI declares moral opposition to slavery and the slave trade.

* * *

Massachusetts repeals its antimiscegenation laws.

The World Anti-Slavery Convention is held in London, attended by prominent American Abolitionists. When women are denied admission, Elizabeth Cady Stanton and William Lloyd Garrison are among those who walk out in protest.

1841

November 7: Sailing from Hampton, Virginia, to New Orleans, the slaveship *Creole* is captured by its slaves, who sail for the Bahamas and freedom.

Frederick Douglass begins his career as a lecturer with the Massachusetts Anti-Slavery Society.

1842

March 1: The U.S. Supreme Court rules, in *Prigg v. Commonwealth of Pennsylvania*, that a state cannot prohibit enforcement of the Fugitive Slave Act of 1793.

March 21–23: Angered by Joshua Giddings's Abolitionist position, Southern congressmen obtain a majority and vote to censure Giddings. He resigns on March 23, is reelected in April, and takes his seat again on May 8.

1843

January: Dorothea Dix addresses the Massachusetts legislature on the harsh and abusive treatment of the mentally ill.

Newly settled German Jews in New York City found the organization B'nai B'rith.

1844

Angered by the influx of Irish Catholics, New Yorkers elect a "nativist" mayor.

December 3: House of Representatives lifts "gag rule" prohibiting slavery debate.

Divided over the slavery issue, the Baptist Church splits into Northern and Southern conventions.

1845

The Methodist Church divides over the slavery issue.

Margaret Fuller writes her *Woman in the Nineteenth Century*, which becomes a classic feminist work.

In Worcester, Massachusetts, Macon B. Allen becomes the first black American admitted to the bar.

1846

May 13: United States declares war on Mexico, largely over the U.S. right to annex Texas. The war intensifies the slavery debate and regional differences. Southerners see Mexican Territory as a place to extend slavery; Northerners oppose such actions.

December 28: Iowa enters the Union as a free state.

1847

Dred Scott files his first suit for freedom in the Circuit Court of St. Louis, Missouri.

The Vermont legislature passes a law allowing married women to retain ownership of property held at time of marriage, with husband's consent still needed for transfer.

Frederick Douglass begins publication of his Abolitionist newspaper, the *North Star*.

November: The Abolitionist Liberty party nominates John P. Hale for president.

1848

February 2: Treaty of Guadalupe Hidalgo ends U.S. war with Mexico.

* * *

July 19–21: First Women's Rights Convention in Seneca Falls is chaired by Lucretia Mott and Elizabeth Cady Stanton. Susan B. Anthony attends. Property rights, divorce, and suffrage are discussed. Using the Declaration of Independence as a model, the convention adopts a Declaration of Sentiments and Resolutions calling for political, social, and economic emancipation of women.

FROM THE SENECA FALLS DECLARATION OF SENTIMENTS

The history of mankind is a history of repeated injuries and usurpations on the part of man toward woman, having in direct object the establishment of an absolute tyranny over her. To prove this, let the facts be submitted to a candid world.

He has never permitted her to exercise her inalienable right to the elective franchise.

He has compelled her to submit to laws, in the formation of which she had no voice.

He has withheld from her rights which are given to the most ignorant and degraded men—both natives and foreigners.

Having deprived her of this first right of a citizen, the elective franchise, thereby leaving her without representation in the halls of legislation, he has oppressed her on all sides.

He has made her, if married, in the eye of the law, civilly dead.

He has taken from her all right in property, even to the wages she earns.

He has made her, morally, an irresponsible being, as she can commit many crimes with impunity, provided they be done in the presence of her husband. In the covenant of marriage, she is compelled to promise obedience to her husband, he becoming, to all intents and purposes, her master—the law giving him power to deprive her of her liberty, and to administer chastisement. . . .

Resolutions

Resolved, That such laws as conflict, in any way, with the true and substantial happiness of woman, are contrary to the great precept of nature, and of no validity; for this is "superior in obligation to any other."

Resolved, That all laws which prevent women from occupying such a station in society as her conscience shall dictate, or which place her in a position inferior to that of man, are contrary to the great precept of nature, and therefore of no force or authority.

Resolved, That woman is man's equal—was intended to be so by the Creator, and the highest good of the race demands that she should be recognized as such. . . .

Resolved, That woman has too long rested satisfied in the circumscribed limits which corrupt customs and a perverted application of the Scriptures have marked out for her, and that it is time she should move in the enlarged sphere which her great Creator has assigned her.

Resolved, That it is the duty of the women of this country to secure to themselves their sacred right to the elective franchise.

Resolved, That the equality of human rights results necessarily from the fact of the identity of the race in capabilities and responsibilities. . . .

Resolved, That the speedy success of our cause depends upon the zealous and untiring efforts of both men and women, for the overthrow of the monopoly of the pulpit, and for the securing to woman an equal participation with men in the various trades, professions and commerce.

1849

First issue of *Lily*, the influential feminist bimonthly published by Amelia Bloomer, women's suffrage and temperance advocate.

September–November: California adopts a constitution prohibiting slavery.

Harriet Tubman escapes from slavery. Once free, Tubman establishes an underground railroad to smuggle fugitive slaves into the north. Risking life and liberty, she makes at least 19 trips back to the South and smuggles over 300 slaves across the border.

Publication of Henry David Thoreau's "Civil Disobedience." He calls on readers to resist a government that protects slavery and invades Mexico. The essay shows the moral indignation of Abolitionists and others, who feel that America has strayed far from its founding principles.

From "Civil Disobedience"

How does it become a man to behave toward this American government to-day? I answer that he cannot without disgrace be associated with it. I cannot for an instant recognize that political organization as my government which is the slave's government also.

All men recognize the right of revolution; that is, the right to refuse allegiance to and to resist the government, when its tyranny or its inefficiency are great and unendurable. But almost all say that such is not the case now. But such was the case, they think, in the Revolution of '75. If one were to tell me that this was a bad government because it taxed certain foreign commodities brought to its ports, it is most probable that I should not make an ado about it, for I can do without them; all machines have their friction; and possibly this does enough good to counterbalance the evil. At any rate, it is a great evil to make a stir about it. But when the friction comes to have its machine, and oppression and robbery are organized, I say, let us not have such a machine any longer. In other words, when a sixth of the population of a nation which has undertaken to be the refuge of liberty are slaves, and a whole country is unjustly overrun and conquered by a foreign army, and subject to military law, I think that it is not too soon for honest men to rebel and revolutionize.

What makes this duty the more urgent is the fact, that the country so overrun is not our own, but ours is the invading army. . . .

1850

September 18: Henry Clay's "Compromise of 1850" allows California to enter the Union as a free state. New Mexico and Utah territories are established without restrictions on slavery. Slavery is banned in the District of Columbia. A strengthened Fugitive Slave Act now requires return of escaped slaves to owners and offers federal officers a fee for each slave returned.

October 23–24: Women's Rights Convention convenes in Worcester, Massachusetts, with delegates from nine states.

November 11–18: Leaders from nine Southern states convene in Nashville to discuss the right of secession.

December 14: Georgia state convention declares its intention to secede if Northern states do not adhere to "Compromise of 1850."

1851

Amelia Bloomer popularizes pants for women. Designed to liberate females from corsets and yards of fabric, these "bloomers" enjoy a short-lived and scandalous popularity.

February 15: Shadrach, a fugitive slave, is rescued from agents by an angry Boston mob, sparking a nationwide furor over enforcement of the new Fugitive Slave Law.

June 15: *Uncle Tom's Cabin*, by Harriet Beecher Stowe, begins serialization in the anti-slavery Washington, D.C., newspaper, *National Era*.

December 1: Abolitionist Charles Sumner fills Daniel Webster's seat in the Senate.

May 29: Former slave Sojourner Truth delivers a moving speech to the Ohio Women's Rights Convention in Akron, demonstrating the double burden of being black and a woman in the United States.

From Sojourner Truth's Address to the Ohio Women's Rights Convention

That man over there says that women need to be helped into carriages and lifted over ditches, and to have the best place everywhere. Nobody ever helps me into carriages or over mud puddles, or gives me any best place. And ain't I a woman? Look at me! I have ploughed and planted and gathered into barns and no man could head me. And ain't I a woman? I could work as much and eat as much as a man—when I could get it—and hear the lash as well. And ain't I a woman? I have borne thirteen children and seen most all sold off to slavery, and when I cried out with my mother's grief, none but Jesus heard me. And ain't I a woman?

Then they talk about this thing in the head; What's that they call it? [Intellect, whispers someone.] That's it, honey. What's that got to do with women's rights or negroes' rights? If my cup won't hold but a pint and yours holds a quart, wouldn't you be mean not to let my little half-measure full.

Then that little man in back there, he says women can't have as much rights as men 'cause Christ wasn't a woman. Where did your Christ come from? From God and a woman! Man had nothing to do with Him.

If the first woman God ever made was strong enough to turn the world upside down all alone, these women together ought to be able to turn it back, and get it right side up again! And now they is asking to do it, the men better let them.

1852

March 20: *Uncle Tom's Cabin* is published in book form. Stowe hopes that the book will show slaveholders the sinfulness of slavery and force them to abandon the institution. The book sells 300,000 copies in one year in the United States alone, and over 1.5 million in England. More influential than any Abolitionist document, this sentimental novel galvanizes Northerners against the evils of slavery, and the enforcement of the Fugitive Slave Law in particular.

August 23: *Uncle Tom's Cabin* opens as a stage play at the National Theatre in New York City.

October 26: Massachusetts Senator Charles Sumner delivers a four-hour speech condemning the Fugitive Slave Law.

July 4: Frederick Douglass delivers a scathing Independence Day address in Rochester, New York. Editor of the *North Star*, and organizer of the underground railroad smuggling fugitive slaves into Canada, Douglass is one of the leading lights of the Abolitionist movement.

FROM FREDERICK DOUGLASS'S JULY 4 ADDRESS

Fellow citizens: Pardon me, and allow me to ask, why am I called upon to speak here today? What have I or those I represent to do with your national independence? Are the great principles of political freedom and of natural justice, embodied in that Declaration of Independence, extended to us? And am I, therefore, called upon to bring our humble offering to the national altar, and to confess the benefits, and express devout gratitude for the blessing resulting from your independence to us? . . .

What to the American slave is your Fourth of July? I

answer, a day that reveals to him more than all other days of the year, the gross injustice and cruelty to which he is the constant victim. To him your celebration is a sham; your boasted liberty an unholy license; your national greatness, swelling vanity; your sounds of rejoicing are empty and heartless; your denunciation of tyrants, brass-fronted impudence; your shouts of liberty and equality, hollow mockery; your prayers and hymns, your sermons and thanksgivings, with all your religious parade and solemnity, are to him mere bombast, fraud, deception, impiety, and hypocrisy—a thin veil to cover up crimes which would disgrace a nation of savages. There is not a nation of the earth guilty of practices more shocking and bloody than are the people of these United States at this very hour.

Go where you may, search where you will, roam through all the monarchies and despotisms of the Old World, travel through South America, search out every abuse and when you have found the last, lay your facts by the side of the everyday practices of this nation, and you will say with me that, for revolting barbarity and shameless hypocrisy, America reigns without a rival. . . .

1854

January 4: Illinois Senator Stephen A. Douglas proposes the Kansas-Nebraska Act, allowing both states to determine their slavery status by popular vote. This bill effectively nullifies the Missouri Compromise.

* * *

February 28: Anti-slavery opponents of the Kansas-Nebraska Act meet in Ripon, Wisconsin, and establish the Republican party.

May 26–June 2: The Senate passes the Kansas-Nebraska Act. In protest, anti-slavery crusader Wendell Phillips leads a group of Abolitionists in an attack on the federal court house in Boston, in an attempt to free the fugitive slave Anthony Burns. Thousands of troops and police are needed to return Burns to Virginia. Burns is eventually sold to people in Boston, who set him free.

October 4: Abraham Lincoln delivers a speech in Springfield, Illinois attacking the Kansas-Nebraska Act, and urging gradual emancipation.

November: The convention of the nativist American, or Know-Nothing, party meets in Cincinnati, Ohio. The party extols the virtues of native-born Protestants, and proposes a 21-year residency requirement for citizenship and exclusion of Catholics and foreigners from public office.

1855

Frederick Douglass publishes his autobiography, *My Bondage and My Freedom*.

* * *

October: Lucy Stone addresses the Women's Rights Convention in Cincinnati, Ohio. Even many of the most progressive reformers of the 1850s show their discomfort with feminism. When one male speaker characterizes feminists as "disappointed women," Lucy Stone is quick to respond.

FROM LUCY STONE'S ADDRESS ON "DISAPPOINTED WOMEN"

The last speaker alluded to this movement as being that of a few disappointed women. From the first years to which my memory stretches, I have been a disappointed woman. When, with my brothers, I reached forth after the sources of knowledge, I was reproved with "It isn't fit for you; it doesn't belong to women." Then there was but one college in the world where women were admitted, and that was in Brazil. I would have found my way there, but by the time I was prepared to go, one was opened in the young State of Ohio—the first in the United States where women and Negroes could enjoy opportunities with white men. I was disappointed when I came to seek a profession worthy an immortal being— every employment was closed to me, except those of the teacher, the seamstress, and the housekeeper. In education, in marriage, in religion, in everything, disappointment is the lot of women. It shall be the business of my life to deepen this disappointment in every woman's heart until she bows down to it no longer. I wish that women, instead of being walking show-cases, instead of begging of their father and brothers the latest and gayest new bonnet, would ask of them their rights. . . .

Wendell Phillips says, "The best and greatest thing one is capable of doing, that is his sphere." I have confidence in the Father to believe that when He gives us the capacity to do anything He does not make a blunder. Leave women, then, to find their sphere. And do not tell us before we are born even, that our province is to cook dinners, darn stockings, and sew on buttons. . . .

1856

Faced with a dwindling supply of slaves, South Carolina's governor argues for the resumption of the slave trade, outlawed in 1808.

February 22: The Know-Nothing party nominates Millard Fillmore for president.

May 19–22: Three days after delivering a speech vilifying pro-slavery legislators, Senator Charles Sumner of Massachusetts is severely beaten on the floor of the Senate by cane-wielding Representative Preston Brooks of South Carolina.

May 21: Gunfire breaks out between pro- and anti-slavery elements in Lawrence, Kansas, earning the territory the name "Bleeding Kansas."

* * *

June 17–19: The Republican party nominates former California senator John C. Frémont for president.

1857

Hinton Rowan Helper publishes *The Impending Crisis of the South: How to Meet It*, arguing that the institution has impoverished nonslaveholding whites. The book is banned in the South.

Pro-slavery journalist George Fitzhugh of Richmond, Virginia, writes *Cannibals All! or Slaves Without Masters*, arguing that Southern slaveholders are more beneficent than Northern factory owners.

January 15: At the Massachusetts State Disunion Convention, William Lloyd Garrison argues for a peaceful separation of North and South. He proclaims *no union with slaveholders*.

March 6: The Supreme Court, in *Dred Scott v. Sanford*, bolsters slavery's cause by ruling that slaves cannot sue for freedom because they are not citizens. The Court further rules that Congress has no right to regulate the ownership of slave "property" anywhere in the nation.

1858

June 16: The Republican party nominates Abraham Lincoln to challenge Stephen Douglas for his Illinois Senate seat. Lincoln provides a contrast to his compromising opponent. In accepting his nomination, Lincoln states, *I believe this Government cannot endure permanently half-slave and half-free.* Although Lincoln is defeated, his debates with Douglas establish him as a national figure.

1859

October 16–18: Abolitionist John Brown leads an attack on the federal arsenal at Harper's Ferry, Virginia, in an attempt to gain arms in order to form a republic for fugitive slaves in the Appalachians. U.S. Marines capture the raiders, killing several. Brown is hung for treason, conspiracy, and murder on December 2. Reviled as a madman and a terrorist in the South, Brown becomes a martyr for the Abolitionist cause, and the song "John Brown's Body" becomes an anthem for the Union cause during the Civil War.

John A. Copeland, a free black, participates in Brown's raid, is captured, and is sentenced to hang. Awaiting execution, he writes to his family and tells them of his "holy cause."

FROM JOHN A. COPELAND'S LETTER TO HIS FAMILY

Dear Parents,—My fate as far as man can seal it is sealed, but let this not occasion you any misery, for remember the cause in which I was engaged, remember that it was a "Holy Cause," one in which men who in every point of view [were] better than I am have suffered and died. Remember that if I must die I die in trying to liberate a few of my poor and oppressed people from my condition of servitude which God in his Holy Writ has hurled his most bitter denunciations against and in which men who were by the color of their faces removed from the direct injurious effect, have already lost their lives and still more remain to meet the same fate which has been by man decided that I must meet. . . .

I am not terrified by the gallows, which I see staring me in the face, and upon which I am soon to stand and suffer death for doing what George Washington was made a hero for doing. . . . For having lent my aid to a general no less brave, and engaged in a cause no less honorable and glorious, I am to suffer death. Washington entered the field to fight for the freedom of the American people—not for the white man alone, but for both black and white. Nor were they white men alone who fought for the freedom of this country. The blood of black men flowed as freely as that of white men. . . . And some of the very last blood shed was that of black men. . . .

And now, dear brother, could I die in a more noble cause? Could I die in a manner and for a cause which would induce true and honest men more to honor me, and the angels more ready to receive me to their happy home of everlasting joy above?

1860

March 19: Elizabeth Cady Stanton addresses the New York State legislature, which later grants property rights to women.

May 16–18: Abraham Lincoln is nominated by the Republican party on a moderate anti-slavery platform, calling for abolition in the new territories only.

June 18–23: After delegates from eight Southern states withdraw from the convention, the Democratic party nominates Stephen Douglas for president.

June 28: Southern Democrats, calling themselves National Democrats, nominate John C. Breckenridge of Kentucky for president.

November 6: With an electoral majority and a minority of the popular vote, Abraham Lincoln is elected 16th president. Southern secession is all but assured. The 80-year-long attempt to compromise on the slavery issue is over.

December 20: South Carolina votes to secede from the Union.

December 30: The South Carolina State militia seizes the federal arsenal in Charleston.

1861

February 8: After seven Southern states secede from the Union, they establish the Confederate States of America.

March 4: In his inaugural address, Lincoln vows that *I have no purpose . . . to interfere with the institution of slavery.* In the same speech he observes that if war comes, *it will come over secession, not slavery.*

April 12: Confederates fire on Union forces in Fort Sumter, Charleston, South Carolina. The Civil War begins.

The secretary of the navy authorizes enlistment of slaves in this branch of the armed services.

1862

July: Congress passes the Confiscation Act, freeing all slaves whose masters support the Confederacy, and the Militia Act, allowing the president to enlist black men; 180,000 blacks serve in the Union Army, 30,000 in the Navy, and 68,000 are killed or wounded.

July 22: President Lincoln presents to his cabinet his plan for emancipation of slaves in Confederate states.

August 20: In a newspaper editorial "A Prayer of Twenty Millions," Horace Greeley calls for emancipation of all slaves. Lincoln replies in a letter to the *New*

York Tribune, My permanent object . . . is to preserve the union, and it is not either to save or destroy slavery.

September 23: Lincoln's Emancipation Proclamation is published in Northern newspapers.

1863

January 1: Lincoln issues the Emancipation Proclamation, freeing "all slaves in areas still in rebellion." Since it "frees" slaves only in Confederate hands, it is largely symbolic. It does not disturb slavery in crucial pro-Union border states. Nevertheless it officially transforms the reason for the war from an attempt to preserve the Union to a crusade to destroy slavery.

THE EMANCIPATION PROCLAMATION

By The President Of The United States Of America: A Proclamation

Whereas on the 22d day of September, A.D. 1862, a proclamation was issued by the President of the United States, containing, among other things, the following, to wit:

That on the 1st day of January, A.D. 1863, all persons held as slaves within any State or designated part of a State the people whereof shall then be in rebellion against the United States shall be then, thenceforward, and forever free; and the executive government of the United States, including the military and naval authority thereof, will recognize and maintain the freedom of such persons and will do no act or acts to repress such persons, or any of them, in any efforts they may make for their actual freedom. . . .

Now, therefore, I, Abraham Lincoln, President of the United States, by virtue of the Power in me vested as Commander in Chief of the Army and Navy of the United States in time of actual armed rebellion against the authority and government of the United States, and as a fit and necessary war measure for suppressing said rebellion, do, on this 1st day of January, A.D. 1863, and in accordance with my purpose so to do, publicly proclaimed for the full period of one hundred days from the first day above mentioned, order and designate as the States and parts of States wherein the people thereof, respectively, are this day in rebellion against the United States the following, to wit:

[The Confederate states, excepting designated Louisiana parishes, Virginia counties, and the state of Tennessee.]

And by virtue of the power and for the purpose aforesaid, I do order and declare that all persons held as slaves within said designated States and parts of States are, and henceforward shall be, free; and that the Executive Government of the United States, including the military and naval authorities thereof, will recognize and maintain the freedom of said persons.

And I hereby enjoin upon the people so declared to be free to abstain from all violence, unless in necessary self-defense; and I recommend to them that, in all cases when allowed, they labor faithfully for reasonable wages.

And I further declare and make known that such per-

sons of suitable condition will be received into the armed service of the United States to garrison forts, positions, stations, and other places, and to man vessels of all sorts in said service.

And upon this act, sincerely believed to be an act of justice, warranted by the Constitution upon military necessity, I invoke the considerate judgment of mankind and the gracious favor of Almighty God.

July 11–14: Violent draft riots break out in New York City, protesting the unfairness of conscription rules, with mobs venting their anger on blacks.

1864

November 8: Buoyed by Union victories, Lincoln narrowly defeats the Democratic party's peace candidate, George McClellan.

1865

March 4: Lincoln's second inaugural address. With the war all but won, his address aims to heal the wounds of a nation that has lost over 600,000 dead.

FROM LINCOLN'S SECOND INAUGURAL ADDRESS

With malice toward none, with charity for all, with firmness in the right as God gives us to see the right, let us strive on to finish the work we are in, to bind up the nation's wounds, to care for him who shall have borne the battle and for his widow and his orphan, to do all which may achieve and cherish a just and lasting peace among ourselves and with all nations.

April 9: General Lee surrenders to General Grant at Appomattox Court House in Virginia, ending the Civil War.

April 14: President Lincoln is assassinated, Washington, D.C.

November 24: The Mississippi legislature passes the "black codes," limiting the civil rights of newly freed slaves. Blacks are prohibited from testifying in court against whites, attending schools with whites, and sitting on juries. Unemployed blacks are subject to arrest for vagrancy.

December 5–14: Congress refuses to seat representatives from former Confederate states, many of whom were active in the rebellion. The House and Senate establish a joint committee on Reconstruction.

December 18: The 13th Amendment to the U.S. Constitution, outlawing slavery throughout the country, is ratified.

THE 13TH AMENDMENT

1. Neither slavery nor involuntary servitude, except as a punishment for crime whereof the party shall have been duly convicted, shall exist within the United States or any place subject to their jurisdiction.

2. Congress shall have power to enforce this article by appropriate legislation.

December 24: The Ku Klux Klan is founded in Pulaski, Tennessee, organized to oppress and terrorize newly enfranchised blacks.

1866

February 19: In response to black codes and Klan activity, Congress votes to strengthen the Freedmen's Bureau. President Johnson vetoes the bill, and calls on freed blacks to help themselves. Congress overrides the veto on July 10.

April 9: Congress passes the Civil Rights Act of 1866, over President Johnson's veto. This law puts the federal government squarely behind the enforcement of equal rights for former slaves.

June 16: Congress proposes the 14th Amendment.

July 30: Inclusion of black suffrage in the Louisiana state constitution sparks riots in New Orleans, killing hundreds of blacks and whites.

* * *

November: Republicans sweep congressional elections, ensuring veto-proof control of Reconstruction policy. Edward G. Walker and Charles L. Mitchell are elected to the Massachusetts House of Representatives as the first black state legislators.

1867

March 2: Congress passes the first Reconstruction Act, providing for military rule in former Confederate states; 20,000 troops are sent to occupy Southern states. Ratification of 14th Amendment becomes a condition for readmission to the Union. There are 600,000 black voters now registered, enabling blacks to elect representatives for the first time. Many Northerners referred to as "carpetbaggers" enter the South to exploit the political and economic chaos. Long derided as a time of corruption, the Reconstruction Era is an attempt at nothing less than a social revolution.

1868

June 22–25: Arkansas, Alabama, Florida, Georgia, Louisiana, North Carolina, and South Carolina are readmitted to the Union.

July 28: The 14th Amendment is ratified, defining citizenship and guaranteeing that all citizens are entitled to "due process of law." It also gives the federal government the right to intervene if states or local governments deprive citizens of their rights. This crucial amendment redefines the relationship between the federal government and the states, and, when enforced, becomes the basis for most of the civil rights legislation that follows in the next 100 years.

THE 14TH AMENDMENT

1. All persons born or naturalized in the United States, and subject to the jurisdiction thereof, are citizens of the United States and of the State wherein they reside. No State shall make or enforce any law which shall abridge the privileges or immunities of citizens of the United States; nor shall any State deprive any person of life, liberty, or property, without due process of law; nor deny to any person within its jurisdiction the equal protection of the laws.

2. Representatives shall be apportioned among the several States according to their respective numbers, counting the whole number of persons in each State, excluding Indians not taxed. But when the right to vote at any election for the choice of Electors for President and Vice-President of the United States, Representatives in Congress, the executive and judicial officers of a State, or the members of the Legislature thereof, is denied to any of the male inhabitants of such State, being twenty-one years of age, and citizens of the United States, or in any way abridged, except for participation in rebellion, or other crime, the basis of representation therein shall be reduced in the proportion which the number of such male citizens shall bear to the whole number of male citizens twenty-one years of age in such State.

3. No person shall be a Senator or Representative in Congress, or Elector of President and Vice-President, or hold any office, civil or military, under the United States, or under any State, who, having previously taken an oath, as a member of Congress, or as an officer of the United States, or as a member of any State Legislature, or as an executive or judicial officer of any State, to support the Constitution of the United States, shall have engaged in insurrection or rebellion against the same, or given aid or comfort to the enemies thereof. But Congress may by a vote of two-thirds of each House, remove such disability.

4. The validity of the public debt of the United States, authorized by law, including debts incurred for payment of pensions and bounties for services in suppressing insurrection or rebellion, shall not be questioned. But neither the United States nor any State shall assume or pay any debt or obligation incurred in aid of insurrection or rebellion against the United States, or any claim for the loss or emancipation of any slave; but all such debts, obligations and claims, shall be held illegal and void.

5. The Congress shall have power to enforce, by appropriate legislation, the provisions of this article.

In defining citizenship, the 14th Amendment uses the terms "male inhabitants" and "male citizens" in section 2. This is the first time gender is mentioned in the Constitution. Women's rights advocates are outraged. Many had been active in the struggle for black rights and feel that this is an appropriate time for women also to be granted equal rights. Elizabeth Cady Stanton writes, *If that word "male" is inserted now, it will take us a century at least to get it out again.*

September: After Georgia expels blacks from its state legislature, military rule is reimposed.

1869

The National Woman Suffrage Association is founded by Elizabeth Cady Stanton and Susan B. Anthony. Their publication *Revolution* advocates, *Men Their Rights and Nothing More; Women Their Rights and Nothing Less.* While the NWSA calls for the political, economic, and social liberation of women, Lucy Stone establishes the Boston-based American Woman Suffrage Association and its *Woman's Journal*, specifically dedicated to winning the vote.

January 19: American Equal Rights Association meets in Washington, D.C. Susan Brownwell is elected president.

February 27: Congress proposes the 15th Amendment, guaranteeing black male suffrage.

July 13: Anti-Chinese riots break out in San Francisco.

* * *

December 10: Wyoming Territory passes the first law giving women the right to vote.

December 22: Congress makes ratification of the 15th Amendment a condition for Georgia's readmission to the Union.

1870

February 12: Utah Territory grants women the right to vote.

February 25: Representative Joseph H. Rainey is seated as the first black in the House of Representatives. Hiram R. Revels becomes the first black senator.

March 30: The 15th Amendment is ratified, guaranteeing all citizens the right to vote.

THE 15TH AMENDMENT

1. The right of citizens of the United States to vote shall not be denied or abridged by the United States or by any State on account of race, color, or previous condition of servitude.

2. The Congress shall have power to enforce this article by appropriate legislation.

* * *

May 31: Passage of enforcement ("Force Act"), or Klu Klux Klan Act, to establish federal supervision of elections, in an attempt to prevent Southern states from infringing on civil rights of black citizens after troops are removed.

Publication of *Joseph and His Friend* by Bayard Taylor, the first American gay novel.

1871

February 28: Faced with challenges to black participation in elections, Congress passes the second "Force Act," the Federal Election Law, providing federal supervision of state and local elections in cities with populations of 20,000 or more.

April 20: Congress enacts its third "Force Act," the Ku Klux Klan Act, specifying procedures and penalties for violations of the 14th Amendment, using military force, if necessary.

October 24: In Los Angeles, 23 Chinese are lynched by white citizens in anti-Chinese riots.

1872

November 5: Susan B. Anthony is arrested while attempting to vote in the presidential election. She is found guilty and fined $100. At her trial, she makes a forceful case for women's rights.

Susan B. Anthony on Women's Rights

As when slaves who got their freedom had to take it over or under or through the unjust forms of the law, precisely now must women take it to get their right to a voice in this government . . . and I shall earnestly and persistently continue to urge all women to the practical recognition of the old Revolutionary maxim, "Resistance to tyranny is obedience to God."

1874

September 17: Riots break out in New Orleans between Southern whites and supporters of a carpetbagger sheriff.

December 7: 70 blacks are killed in rioting in Vicksburg, Mississippi, following rejection by white residents of a carpetbagger sheriff.

1875

March 1: Congress passes the Civil Rights Act of 1875, guaranteeing black Americans equal rights in public places and barring exclusion from juries.

THE CIVIL RIGHTS ACT OF 1875

Whereas it is essential to just government we recognize the equality of all men before the law, and hold that it is the duty of government in its dealings with the people to mete out equal and exact justice to all, of whatever nativity, race, color, or persuasion, religious or political; and it being the appropriate object of legislation to enact great fundamental principles into law: Therefore,

Be it enacted, *That all persons within the jurisdiction of the United States shall be entitled to the full and equal enjoyment of the accommodations, advantages, facilities, and privileges of inns, public conveyances on land or water, theaters, and other places of public amusement; subject only to the conditions and limitations established by law, and applicable alike to citizens of every race and color, regardless of any previous condition of servitude. . . .*

That no citizen possessing all other qualifications which are or may be prescribed by law shall be disqualified for service as grand or petit juror in any court of the United States, or of any State, on account of race, color, or previous condition of servitude; and any officer or other person charged with any duty in the selection or summoning of jurors who shall exclude or fail to summon any citizen for the cause aforesaid shall, on conviction thereof, be deemed guilty of a misdemeanor, and be fined not more than five thousand dollars.

That all cases arising under the provisions of this act . . . shall be renewable by the Supreme Court of the

United States, without regard to the sum in contro-
versy. . . .

1876

November 7: In the presidential election, Democratic
party candidate Samuel Tilden wins a majority of popular
votes, but is denied electoral victory because of disputed
votes in Florida, Louisiana, South Carolina, and Oregon. The election is decided by a commission of congressmen, and Republican Rutherford B. Hayes is
declared president. This decision, known as the "Great
Swap," is the result of a deal that gives Hayes the White
House in return for his promise to remove all military
troops from the South and effectively end Reconstruction. Federal protection of civil rights for former slaves
comes to an end.

1877

April 24: The last federal troops are withdrawn from
New Orleans.

June 15: Henry O. Flipper is first black American to
graduate from the U.S. Military Academy at West Point.

1878

January 10: The Women's Suffrage Amendment is introduced in the Senate by Aaron A. Sargent of California.

Defeated 16-34, this bill is reintroduced each year until it finally passes in 1918.

1879

February 15: Congress enacts a law giving female attorneys the right to argue before the U.S. Supreme Court.

May 7: California adopts new state constitutional provision forbidding employment of Chinese laborers.

June: 7,000 Southern blacks fleeing oppressive conditions attempt to migrate to St. Louis, Missouri, but settle in Kansas. Known as "Exodusters," they are provided shelter and hospitality by the state of Kansas.

1880

March 1: In *Strauder v. West Virginia*, the U.S. Supreme Court rules that the 14th Amendment bans racial discrimination in jury selection.

November 17: The Chinese Exclusion Treaty is signed by China and the United States, giving the country the arbitrary right to limit, regulate, and suspend immigration of Chinese nationals.

1881

Publication of *A Century of Dishonor* by Helen Hunt Jackson, recounting mistreatment of Native Americans at the hands of the U.S. government.

July 4: The Alabama legislature establishes the Tuskegee Normal and Industrial Institute. Booker T. Washington is named president. Washington gains national attention with his efforts to teach vocational and industrial skills to newly freed blacks and sharecroppers. Beginning with a $2000 donation, Tuskegee becomes the greatest center of vocational training for blacks in the nation.

Tennessee passes the first "Jim Crow" law, requiring segregated railroad cars and public facilities, and setting a pattern for other Southern and border states.

1882

April 4: President Arthur vetoes the Chinese Exclusion Act.

May 6: Congress overrides President Arthur's veto and passes the first Chinese Exclusion Act, barring Chinese immigration for 10 years.

1883

April 28: John F. Slater donates $1 million for eponymous fund to educate emancipated slaves.

* * *

October 15: In a group of decisions known as the civil rights cases, the Supreme Court states that the Civil Rights Act of 1875 is unconstitutional, ruling that only state-sponsored discrimination is forbidden, not that of private citizens or corporations. This decision clears the way for segregation of virtually all public facilities in the "Jim Crow" South. Justice John Harlan dissents, arguing that the decision will have far-reaching, negative effects.

THE CIVIL RIGHTS CASES OF 1882, JUSTICE HARLAN DISSENTING

My brethren say, that when a man has emerged from slavery, and by the aid of beneficent legislation has shaken off the inseparable concomitants of that state, there must be some stage in the progress of his elevation when he takes the rank of a mere citizen, and ceases to be the special favorite of the laws, and when his rights as a citizen, or a man, are to be protected in the ordinary modes by which other men's rights are protected. It is, I submit, scarcely just to say that the colored race has been the special favorite of the laws. The statute of 1875, now adjudged to be unconstitutional, is for the benefit of citizens of every race and color. What the nation, through Congress, has sought to accomplish in reference to that race, is—what had already been done in every State of the Union for the white race—to secure and protect rights

*belonging to them as freemen and citizens; nothing more.
It was not deemed enough "to help the feeble up, but
to support him after." The one underlying purpose of
congressional legislation has been to enable the black
race to take the rank of mere citizens. The difficulty
has been to compel a recognition of the legal right of
the black race to take the rank of citizens, and to secure the enjoyment of privileges belonging, under the
law, to them as a component part of the people for whose
welfare and happiness government is ordained. At every
step, in this direction, the nation has been confronted
with class tyranny, which a contemporary English histo-
rian says is, of all tyrannies, the most intolerable, "for it
is ubiquitous in its operation, and weighs, perhaps, most
heavily on those whose obscurity or distance would withdraw them from the notice of a single despot." To-day,
it is the colored race which is denied, by corporations
and individuals wielding public authority, rights fundamental in their freedom and citizenship. At some future
time, it may be that some other race will fall under the
ban of race discrimination. If the constitutional amendments be enforced, according to the intent with which, as
I conceive, they were adopted, there cannot be, in this
republic, any class of human being in practical subjection
to another class, with power in the latter to dole out to
the former just such privileges as they may choose to
grant. . . .*

*For the reasons stated I feel constrained to withhold
my assent to the opinion of the court.*

1884

Women's suffrage activists form the "National Equal Rights" party, and nominate Belva A. Lockwood for president. A lawyer, Lockwood was the first woman to argue before the Supreme Court (1879).

1886

February 7: In Seattle, violent riots force more than 400 Chinese laborers from their homes. Federal troops are called in.

May 10: In *Yick Wo v. Hopkins*, the Supreme Court rules that aliens have rights as a person, and that a local ordinance against Chinese laundries violates the 14th Amendment.

May 10: The Supreme Court, in *Santa Clara County v. Southern Pacific Railroad*, rules that the 14th Amendment gives corporations the same rights to due process as to individuals.

1888

May 18: The national convention of the Equal Rights party meets in Des Moines, Iowa, and nominates Belva Lockwood for president.

1890

February 18: A merger of the New York and Boston wings of the women's suffrage movement forms the National American Women Suffrage Association. Elizabeth Cady Stanton is elected president.

July 10: After insisting that its suffrage law remain in effect, Wyoming enters the Union as the first state granting women the right to vote.

November 1: Mississippi constitutional convention begins systematic exclusion of black voters by enacting laws requiring black voters to prove the ability to read and understand technical points of constitutional law. Similar laws are adopted by seven other Southern states by 1910, effectively ending black suffrage.

1892

May 5: The Geary Chinese Exclusion Act provides for additional regulation of Chinese laborers and deportation of "unauthorized" aliens, and also extends the immigration ban for an additional 10 years.

1893

May 15: The Supreme Court rules that the Geary Act is unconstitutional.

1894

March 17: The United States and China sign the Chinese Exclusion Treaty, formally agreeing to exclusion of Chinese immigration into the United States. The Senate ratifies the treaty on August 13.

1895

Publication of *The Woman's Bible*, by Elizabeth Cady Stanton, which analyzes and reinterprets derogatory references to women in the Bible.

September: At the Cotton States Exposition in Atlanta, Georgia, Booker T. Washington delivers a speech exhorting his fellow blacks to work hard within the social structure of the South, and for Southerners to give blacks a chance to work. For many blacks, Washington's speech is nothing more than accommodation to the hateful ostracism of Jim Crow. For others, it is practical advice for a people and a region emerging from the near feudal state of slavery.

FROM BOOKER T. WASHINGTON'S ADDRESS

The wisest among my race understand that the agitation of questions of social equality is the extremest folly, and that progress in the enjoyment of all privileges that will come to us must be the result of severe and constant struggle rather than of artificial forcing. No race that has anything to contribute to the markets of the world is long in any degree ostracized. It is important and right that all privileges of the law be ours, but it is vastly more important that we be prepared for the exercise of those privileges. The opportunity to earn a dollar in a factory just now is worth infinitely more than the opportunity to spend a dollar in an opera house.

1896

January 4: Utah enters the Union, and makes women's suffrage part of its new constitution.

May 18: The Supreme Court, in *Plessy v. Ferguson*, gives legal status to the "separate but equal" philosophy of the South's Jim Crow laws. Once again Justice Harlan dissents, in an opinion that will influence future civil rights rulings.

FROM PLESSY V. FERGUSON, JUSTICE HARLAN DISSENTING

The white race deems itself to be the dominant race in this country. And so it is, in prestige, in achievements, in education, in wealth and in power. So, I doubt not, it will continue to be for all time, if it remains true to its great heritage and holds fast to the principles of constitutional liberty. But in view of the Constitution, in the eye of the law, there is in this country no superior, dominant, ruling class of citizens. There is no caste here. Our Consti-

tution is color-blind, and neither knows nor tolerates classes among citizens. In respect of civil rights, all citizens are equal before the law. The humblest is the peer of the most powerful. The law regards man as man, and takes no account of his surroundings or of his color when his civil rights as guaranteed by the supreme law of the land are involved. It is, therefore, to be regretted that this high tribunal, the final expositor of the fundamental law of the land, has reached the conclusion that it is competent for a State to regulate the enjoyment by citizens of their civil rights solely upon the basis of race. . . .

If evils will result from the commingling of the two races upon public highways established for the benefit of all, they will be infinitely less than those that will surely come from state legislation regulating the enjoyment of civil rights upon the basis of race. We boast of the freedom enjoyed by our people above all other peoples. But it is difficult to reconcile that boast with a state of the law which, practically, puts the brand of servitude and degradation upon a large class of our fellow-citizens, our equals before the law. The thin disguise of "equal" accommodations for passengers in railroad coaches will not mislead any one, nor atone for the wrong this day done. . . .

1897

March 2: President Grover Cleveland vetoes an immigration bill requiring a literacy test, stating that it is *a radical departure from our national policy.*

1898

May 28: The Supreme Court declares that native citizenship is without regard to creed or color; it bans deportation of U.S.-born Chinese children, and declares them U.S. citizens.

1900

July 5: At the Democratic national convention, Elizabeth Cohen delivers the seconding speech for Williams Jenning Bryan.

1901

November 28: Alabama's new state constitution disenfranchises black voters by its requiring literacy tests and its "grandfather clause" that limits suffrage to those citizens whose grandfathers had voted.

1902

April 29: The Chinese Exclusion Act is revised to bar Chinese from the Philippines, a new U.S. possession.

1905

Black intellectuals from 14 states, led by W. E. B. Du-Bois, form the Niagara Movement to oppose the conciliatory philosophy of Booker T. Washington and to end all distinctions based on race.

FROM THE NIAGARA MOVEMENT DECLARATION OF PRINCIPLES

Protest: *We refuse to allow the impression to remain that the Negro-American assents to inferiority, is submissive under oppression and apologetic before insults. Through helplessness we may submit, but the voice of protest of ten million Americans must never cease to assail the ears of their fellows, so long as America is unjust. . . .*

Any discrimination based simply on race or color is barbarous, we care not how hallowed it be by custom, expediency or prejudice. Differences made on account of ignorance, immorality, or disease are legitimate methods of fighting evil, and against them we have no word of protest; but discriminations based simply and solely on physical peculiarities, place of birth, color of skin, are relics of that unreasoning human savagery of which the world is and ought to be thoroughly ashamed. . . .

We protest against the "Jim Crow" car, since its effect is and must be to make us pay first-class fare for third-class accommodations, render us open to insults and discomfort and to crucify wantonly our manhood, womanhood and self-respect. . . .

October 2: In *Ladies Home Journal,* former president Grover Cleveland writes that *sensible and responsible*

*women do not want the vote. The relative positions to be
assumed by men and women . . . were assigned long ago
by a higher intelligence than ours.*

1906

March 13: Susan B. Anthony, 86, dies in Rochester,
New York.

September 22: A race riot in Atlanta, Georgia, results in
12 deaths; the city is placed under martial law.

1907

February 20: Congress passes the Immigration Act of
1907, giving the president the power to restrict Japanese
immigration.

March 14: Japanese immigration to the United States is
restricted by presidential order.

1908

January 21: New York City passes the Sullivan ordinance, making it illegal for women to smoke in public.

February 18: U.S and Japan reach an agreement restricting Japanese emigration to the United States.

1909

February 12: The National Association for the Advancement of Colored People (NAACP) is founded, lead by Oswald Garrison Villard, grandson of William Lloyd Garrison. Other founding members include Jane Addams, John Dewey, W. E. B. Dubois, William Dean Howells, and Lincoln Steffens.

1910

The National League on Urban Conditions Among Negroes, later the National Urban League, is formed by business, labor, civic, and religious leaders.

November 8: Washington State passes a constitutional amendment giving women the vote.

1913

March 3: Led by Alice Paul, 10,000 marchers demonstrate in Washington, D.C., on behalf of women's suffrage.

May 5: Helen Keller proclaims public support for the suffrage movement and states that women *cannot hope to get anything unless they are willing to fight and suffer for it.*

June 12: Illinois passes a women's suffrage bill.

1914

June 30: President Wilson declares that women's suffrage should be decided by the states, not via a constitutional amendment.

1915

January 2: President Wilson vetoes an immigration bill containing a provision requiring literacy tests.

Margaret Sanger is charged with obscenity for her how-to pamphlet, "Family Limitations," a pioneering work on birth control.

February 8: D. W. Griffith's film *Birth of a Nation* sparks nationwide protests by black leaders. The film romanticizes the rise of the Ku Klux Klan. President Wilson arranges for a White House screening, and praises the film.

September 16: Suffragist Sara B. Field gathers 500,000 signatures to support a women's suffrage amendment.

December 4: Georgia grants a new charter to a revived Ku Klux Klan.

Two million Southern blacks begin a "Great Migration" to Northern industrial states.

*   *   *

July 21: In *Guinn and Beal v. United States*, the Supreme Court strikes down the "grandfather clause" in the Oklahoma state constitution.

1916

February 11: Anarchist Emma Goldman is arrested for speaking in public about birth control.

October 16: In Brooklyn, New York, Margaret Sanger, Fania Mindell, and Ethel Byrne open the nation's first birth control clinic.

1917

February 5: Congress overrides President Wilson's veto and enacts an immigration law requiring literacy tests for all new arrivals, and bans all Asian immigration except from nations covered by preexisting treaties.

August 28: Ten suffragettes are arrested in front of the White House; 41 are arrested when picketing resumes on November 10.

November 6: The New York State legislature passes a women's suffrage amendment to its constitution.

In New York City, 10,000 march on Fifth Avenue to protest lynchings in Southern states. Marchers include W. E. B. DuBois and James Weldon Johnson.

1918

January 10: The House of Representatives votes 274-136 to pass the women's suffrage amendment. The bill is introduced by Jeannette Rankin of Montana, the first elected woman representative.

September 30: President Wilson speaks to the Senate in favor of the suffrage amendment as a *necessary war measure*.

1919

June 4: Congress sends the 19th Amendment to the states for ratification.

In Paris, W. E. B. DuBois organizes the first Pan-African Congress. Writing in the NAACP's journal, *The Crisis*, DuBois reflects on the feelings of black soldiers returning from the battlefields of World War I.

W. E. B. DuBois on the Black Veterans of World War I

We are returning from War! The Crisis and tens of thousands of black men were drafted into a great struggle. For bleeding France and what she means and has meant and will mean to us and humanity and against the threat of German race arrogance, we fought gladly and to the last drop of blood; for America and her highest ideals, we fought in far-off hope; for the dominant southern oligarchy entrenched in Washington, we fought in bitter resignation. For the America that represents and gloats in lynching, disenfranchisement, caste, brutality and devilish insult—for this, in the hateful upturning and mixing of things, we were forced by vindictive fate to fight. . . .

This is the country to which we Soldiers of Democracy return. This is the fatherland for which we fought! But it is our fatherland. It was right for us to fight. The faults of our country are our faults. Under similar circumstances, we would fight again. But by the God of Heaven, we are cowards and jackasses if now that that war is over, we do not marshal every ounce of our brain and brawn to fight a sterner, longer, more unbending battle against the forces of hell in our land.

We return.

We return from fighting.

We return fighting.

Make way for Democracy! We saved it in France, and by the Great Jehovah, we will save it in the United States of America, or know the reason why.

1920

Marcus Garvey opens an international convention of the Universal Negro Improvement Association in Harlem, New York City.

August 26: The 19th Amendment is ratified, giving women the vote.

* * *

THE 19TH AMENDMENT

1. The right of citizens of the United States to vote shall not be denied or abridged by the United States or by any State on account of sex.

2. Congress shall have power to enforce this Article by appropriate legislation.

1921

May 19: President Harding signs into law a restrictive immigration act favoring immigration from northern Europe.

April 22: A New York physician is fined for publishing and distributing *Love in Marriage*, by Marie C. Stopes, an advocate of birth control.

June 20: Oklahoma Representative Alice Robertson becomes the first woman to preside over the House of Representatives.

November 2: The American Birth Control League is organized under the leadership of Margaret Sanger.

1922

February 27: In a unanimous decision, the Supreme Court finds the 19th Amendment constitutional.

* * *

October 3: Journalist Rebecca Felton of Georgia becomes the first woman U.S. senator, filling the seat of Thomas E. Watson, deceased. She serves for two days.

1923

Alice Paul drafts the Equal Rights Amendment (ERA). This bill is introduced into Congress every year until it is passed by both Houses in 1972.

September 15: Governor John Calloway Walton of Oklahoma places the state under martial law to combat terrorist activities of a revived Ku Klux Klan.

1924

June 24: For the first time, women attend the party national conventions as delegates.

In Illinois, Henry Gerber forms the Society for Human Rights, the first known homosexual organization in the United States. It is broken up by the police after a few weeks of existence.

1925

January 5: Nellie Tayloe Ross of Wyoming becomes the nation's first woman governor.

* * *

August 8: 40,000 members of the Klu Klux Klan demonstrate in Washington, D.C.

1929

In *Nixon v. Herndon*, the U.S. Supreme Court strikes down a Texas law barring blacks from voting in a "white primary," citing a violation of the 14th Amendment.

1928

June 17–18: Amelia Earhart is the first woman to fly across the Atlantic, as a passenger.

November 6: Herbert Hoover is elected president, defeating Alfred E. Smith in an election marred by vicious anti-Catholic attacks against Smith.

1929

The Well of Loneliness by Radcliffe Hall is published, an early, influential lesbian novel that expressed the isolation and alienation of many of its readers. It is soon declared obscene in both the United States and England.

FROM THE WELL OF LONELINESS

You're neither unnatural, nor abominable, nor mad; you're as much a part of what people call nature as anyone else; only you're unexplained as yet—you've not got your niche in creation. But someday that will come, and meanwhile don't shrink from yourself, but face yourself calmly and bravely. . . . But above all be honorable.

April 15: Margaret Sanger's Birth Control Clinical Research Bureau is raided by New York City police at the behest of the Daughters of the American Revolution. The resulting public outcry wins new support for the clinic. The case is dismissed in May.

1931

March 25: In Scottsboro, Alabama, nine black youths are arrested for raping a white woman. Tried and found guilty, their conviction will be overturned in 1935. The trial of the "Scottsboro Boys" brings nationwide attention to the civil injustice of the Jim Crow South.

1932

May 20–21: Amelia Earhart is the first woman to fly solo across the Atlantic.

1933

March 4: Frances Perkins is appointed secretary of labor by President Roosevelt, becoming the first woman to hold a cabinet position.

1937

March 29: The Supreme Court, in *West Coast Hotel v. Parrish*, upholds the minimum wage law for women.

1939

Denied the use of Constitutional Hall by the Daughters of the American Revolution, black singer Marian Anderson performs before an audience of 75,000 assembled at the Lincoln Memorial.

1941

April 28: In a case brought by Congressman Arthur Mitchell, the Supreme Court rules that separate facilities in railroad travel must be *substantially* equal.

June 25: Faced with widespread demonstrations, President Roosevelt establishes the Fair Employment Practices Committee to prevent discrimination at defense-related plants, and issues Executive Order 8802 barring racial discrimination in the defense industry.

1942

January 14: FDR issues a proclamation calling for registration of all aliens.

The Congress of Racial Equality (CORE) is founded to undertake direct-action projects to improve race relations.

* * *

February 19: President Roosevelt issues Executive Order 9066, establishing the War Relocation Authority. As a result, 110,000 Japanese, many of whom are U.S. citizens, are sent to internment camps for the remainder of the war.

May 14: The Women's Army Auxiliary Corp is established by Congress. The name is shorted to Women's Army Corp (WACS) in 1943.

July 30: The Women Appointed for Voluntary Emergency Service (WAVES) is established as part of the U.S. Naval Reserve.

November 23: The Semper Paratas Always Ready Service (SPARS) is organized as the women's branch of the Coast Guard.

1943

June 20: When white workers protest the hiring of black laborers in Detroit, riots break out, leaving 34 dead.

December 17: The Chinese Exclusion Act is repealed.

1944

April 3: The Supreme Court, in *Smith v. Allwright*, declares that all-white primaries are illegal.

1946

January 12: The Supreme Court, in *Morgan v. Commonwealth*, rules that segregation on interstate bus travel is unconstitutional.

1947

Sponsored by President Truman, the Commission on Civil Rights issues its report *To Preserve These Rights*, condemning racial injustice in America.

Jackie Robinson is signed with the Brooklyn Dodgers, becoming the first black man to play major-league baseball. Other black players are signed later in the year in both the National and American leagues, ending the racial segregation of "America's pastime."

1948

January 12: In *Sipeul v. Board of Regents of University of Oklahoma*, the Supreme Court rules that states cannot racially discriminate when choosing law school applicants.

February 2: President Truman submits a civil rights bill to Congress, calling for antilynching laws, abolition of the poll tax, and an end to segregation in education and employment.

March 5: Former Labor Secretary Frances Perkins states that *unless a woman can earn $4000 a year . . . it is absurd, anti-social, and uneconomic for her to work outside the home.*

May 3: In *Shelley v. Kraemer*, the Supreme Court rules that federal and state courts may not enforce restrictive covenants.

The California Supreme Court declares unconstitutional a state law barring racial intermarriage.

Gore Vidal's *The City and the Pillar* is published. The novel is popular and critically acclaimed, frank in its depiction of homosexuality.

July 1: Eleanor Roosevelt ends speculation that she might run as Truman's running mate.

July 17: At its national convention, the Democratic party adopts a strong civil rights platform. Southern delegates (known as Dixiecrats) later bolt to form the States Rights party. The party's civil rights platform is enthusiastically introduced by Hubert H. Humphrey, mayor of Minneapolis and future U.S. senator and later vice-president.

From Hubert H. Humphrey's Address to the 1948 Democratic Convention

There are those who say to you—we are rushing this issue of civil rights. I say we are 172 years too late.

There are those who say—this issue of civil rights is an infringement on states' rights. The time has come for the Democratic party to get out of the shadow of states' rights and walk forthrightly into the bright sunshine of human rights. . . .

For all of us here, for the millions who have sent us, for the whole two billion members of the human family— our land is now, more than ever, the last best hope on earth. I know that we can—I know that we shall—begin here the fuller and richer realization of that hope—that promise of a land where all men are free and equal, and each man uses his freedom and equality wisely and well.

July 28: President Truman issues Executive Order 9981, ending racial segregation in the armed forces.

November 2: Truman is elected in his own right.

1950

January 25: The Senate passes the Equal Rights Amendment, 63-19.

May 24: The *Wall Street Journal* reports that women constitute 29% of the U.S. work force.

Androgynous Anonymous, later named the Mattachine Society, is formed in Los Angeles. This group, organized by former Communist party members Harry Hay, Chuck Rowland, and Bob Hull, will become the most active and public political gay organization in the 1950s and 1960s. In its 1951 statement of purpose, the Mattachine Society pledges to: *unify those homosexuals isolated from their own kind . . . to educate [society] towards an ethical homosexual culture . . . paralleling the emerging cultures of our fellow-minorities—the Negro, Mexican, and Jewish Peoples . . . to assist our people who are victimized daily as a result of our oppression.*

1951

The book *The Homosexual in America*, by Donald Webster Cory, is published. It makes a plea for tolerance.

1952

The Tuskeegee Institute reports that for the first time in 71 years of tabulation, no lynchings have occurred in the United States during the past year.

July 21: At the Republican party's national convention, the GOP affirms support for the Equal Rights Amendment (ERA) in its party platform.

1953

Publication begins of ONE Magazine, an openly gay magazine.

1954

May 17: The Supreme Court, in *Brown v. The Board of Education of Topeka*, rules that racial segregation in public education is unconstitutional.

FROM CHIEF JUSTICE EARL WARREN'S DECISION IN
Brown v. The Board of Education of Topeka

We conclude that in the field of public education the doctrine of "separate but equal" has no place. Separate educational facilities are inherently unequal. Therefore, we hold that the plaintiffs and others similarly situated for whom the actions have been brought are, by reason of the segregation complained of, deprived of the equal protection of the laws guaranteed by the Fourteenth Amendment.

Thurgood Marshall, special counselor to the NAACP, who argued the *Brown* case before the Supreme Court, says that it will take up to five years to end segregation. He predicts that by 1963, the 100th anniversary of the Emancipation Proclamation, segregation in all of its forms will be eliminated.

1955

The lesbian political organization Daughters of Bilitis is founded in San Francisco. In 1958, Barbara Gittings would start the New York City chapter.

* * *

May 31: The Supreme Court bans all segregation in U.S. public schools; it orders schools to desegregate "with all deliberate speed."

November 25: Interstate Commerce Commission bans racial segregation on interstate trains and buses.

December 1: Rosa Parks begins a crusade against Jim Crow laws in Montgomery, Alabama. She is arrested when she refuses to surrender her seat in the front of the bus to a white man.

December 5: After the arrest of Rosa Parks, Martin Luther King, Jr., urges a complete bus boycott. A successful bus boycott ends with complete desegregation in December 1956, and sets a pattern for nonviolent resistance to segregation.

DR. MARTIN LUTHER KING, JR., ON ROSA PARKS

On December 1, 1955, an attractive Negro seamstress, Mrs. Rosa Parks, boarded the Cleveland Avenue bus in downtown Montgomery. She was returning home after her regular day's work in . . . a leading department store. Tired from long hours on her feet, Mrs. Parks sat down in the first seat behind the section reserved for whites. Not long after she took her seat, the bus operator ordered her, along with three other Negro passengers, to move back in order to accommodate boarding white passengers. By this time every seat in the bus was taken. This meant if Mrs. Parks followed the driver's command she would have to stand while a white male passenger, who had just boarded the bus, would sit. The other three Negro passengers immediately complied with the driver's request. But Mrs. Parks quietly refused. The result was her arrest.

There was to be much speculation about why Mrs. Parks did not obey the driver. Many people in the white community argued that she had been "planted" by the NAACP in order to lay the groundwork for a test case.

But the accusation was totally unwarranted. . . . Mrs. Parks' refusal to move back was her own intrepid affirmation that she had had enough. It was an individual expression of a timeless longing for human dignity and freedom. She was not "planted" there by the NAACP, or any other organization; she was planted there by her personal sense of dignity and self-respect.

1956

January 9: To maintain segregation, the Virginia legislature votes to provide funding for private schools.

February 6: Enrollment of black student Autherine Lucy at the University of Alabama provokes three days of riots. Lucy is expelled on March 1.

* * *

February 15: The federal court in New Orleans outlaws all state rulings defying the Supreme Court's desegregation decisions.

March 12: 101 Southern congressmen call for "massive resistance" to the Supreme Court's desegregation rulings.

May 2: The General Council of Methodist Churches votes to abolish segregation within the church.

November 13: The Supreme Court strikes down an Alabama law mandating segregation in interstate travel.

1957

The British government publishes the Wolfenden Report, urging decriminization of homosexual acts.

January: After the successful bus boycott in Montgomery, Dr. Martin Luther King, Jr., emerges as a national figure and the leader of the nonviolent struggle for civil rights. With other Southern black ministers, he organizes the Southern Christian Leadership Council (SCLC) to work with the NAACP and other civil rights organizations to form a united effort to end segregation. He meets with President Eisenhower, Vice-President Nixon and attends the independence ceremonies in the African nation of Ghana. With pride, eloquence and religious fervor, King inspires a generation of blacks and whites committed to change and social justice.

FROM *STRIDE TOWARDS FREEDOM* BY DR. MARTIN LUTHER KING, JR.

Once plagued with a tragic sense of inferiority resulting from the crippling effects of slavery and segregation, the Negro has now been driven to reevaluate himself. He has come to feel that he is somebody. His religion reveals to him that God loves all His children and that the important thing about man is . . . not the color of his skin but his eternal worth to God. . . . There is a new Negro in the South, with a new sense of dignity and destiny.

January 16: President Eisenhower states his personal support for the ERA: *Congress should make certain that women are not denied equal rights with men.*

September 9: President Eisenhower signs the Civil Rights Act of 1957, setting penalties for anyone violating the voting rights of any U.S. Citizen. The bill is the first civil rights bill to pass Congress since Reconstruction.

September 4: Defying the Supreme Court, Arkansas Governor Orval Faubus calls out the state's National Guard to prevent desegregation of Little Rock's schools.

September 20–24: After personal intervention by the president, Governor Faubus removes the National

Guard. President Eisenhower sends 1,000 U.S. troops to Little Rock to enforce school desegregation.

1958

June 29: A bomb explodes outside the church of civil rights leader Fred Shuttleworth.

1959

California repeals its miscegenation laws.

June 18: A federal court strikes down an Arkansas school law used by Governor Faubus to close the schools rather than desegregate.

September 7: The U.S. Civil Rights Commission asks President Eisenhower to appoint federal registrars to oversee voter registration in areas where black registration is challenged.

August 12: Little Rock schools are reopened amid demonstrations.

1960

February 2: College students in Greensboro, North Carolina, begin nonviolent "sit-ins" at segregated lunch counters. This practice spreads throughout the South and eventually results in desegregating public facilities.

* * *

February 29: A filibuster against the new civil rights bill is begun by 18 Southern senators.

April 8: Senate passes Civil Rights Bill 71-18, which clarifies points in the 1957 Civil Rights Act.

May 20: The Southern Baptist Convention passes a resolution questioning the ability of Roman Catholics to hold public office. In an obvious reference to the candidacy of John F. Kennedy, the resolution declares that a Catholic would be too *bound by the dogma and demands of his church* to serve the American public.

September 12: In an address in Houston, John F. Kennedy vows that, if elected president, he will not put the dictates of his church before the duties of his office.

October: Young veterans of the sit-in demonstrations organize the Student Nonviolent Coordinating Committee (SNCC). Marion Barry is the first chairperson. SNCC draws thousands of members from all over the country and proclaims its goals: *to speed up school segregation, to enact fair employment laws, to ensure the right to vote.*

October 26: Dr. Martin Luther King, Jr., is jailed over a traffic violation. Robert Kennedy calls Mrs. King on behalf of his brother.

* * *

November 8: John F. Kennedy is the first Catholic elected president. Despite a lackluster civil rights record, Kennedy receives two-thirds of the black vote, a fact attributed to his personal intervention on behalf of Martin Luther King, Jr.

November 17: 200 people are arrested during anti-integration riots in New Orleans.

1961

Illinois becomes the first state to decriminalize homosexuality between consenting adults.

May 4: 13 "freedom riders" depart on a bus trip from Washington, D.C. to New Orleans. Organized by the Congress of Racial Equality (CORE), this group of seven blacks and six whites set out to test the federal law against segregation in interstate travel. On May 14 their bus is burned outside of Anniston, Alabama. After taking another bus as far as Birmingham, Alabama, they are met by a gang and beaten severely. One rider requires fifty stitches. Despite pleas by Martin Luther King, Jr., and Attorney General Robert Kennedy to turn back, the riders proceed. In Mobile, Alabama, a violent mob attacks the buses as well as reporters and John Siegenthaler, who was sent as an observer by President John Kennedy. Robert Kennedy then orders federal marshals to protect the riders. At Kennedy's request the Interstate

Commerce Commission bans all segregation in interstate bus facilities, effective November 1, 1961.

December 14: President Kennedy issues Executive Order 10980, calling for formation of the Commission on the Status of Women, chaired by Eleanor Roosevelt, to determine ways to eliminate *all barriers to the full partnership of women in our democracy.*

1962

February 26: The Supreme Court rules that segregation in all transportation is unconstitutional, and orders Mississippi bus terminals to desegregate.

April 3: The Defense Department orders integration of all military reserve units.

August 27: Congress approves the 24th Amendment, banning poll taxes in federal elections.

September 28: Mississippi Governor Ross R. Barnett is found guilty of contempt of U.S. Court of Appeals for his efforts to block integration of the University of Mississippi.

October 1: With 3,000 federal troops on hand to quell campus violence, James H. Meredith becomes the first black man to enroll at the University of Mississippi.

* * *

November 30: President Kennedy issues an executive order banning racial segregation in all federally funded housing.

1963

President Kennedy attacks segregation as *morally wrong*.

The Feminine Mystique, by Betty Friedan, is published. Inspired by both the civil rights crusade and the antiwar movement, the women's rights movement of the 1960s and 1970s will address women's social and economic roles. Friedan's lament is the opening salvo in a growing social revolution.

FROM *THE FEMININE MYSTIQUE*

"It . . . is time to stop giving lip service to the idea that there are no battles left to be fought for women in America, that women's rights have already been won. . . . In almost every professional field, women are still treated as second-class citizens. It would be a great service to tell girls who plan to work in society to expect this subtle, uncomfortable discrimination—tell them not to be quiet and hope that it will go away, but fight it. A girl should not expect special privileges because of her sex, but neither should she "adjust" to prejudice and discrimination.

She must learn to compete then, not as a woman, but as a human being. Not until a great many women move out of the fringes into the mainstream will society itself provide the arrangements for this new life plan....

January 28: South Carolina is the last Southern state to integrate its public schools.

April–May: Massive demonstrations protesting racial injustice begin in Birmingham, Alabama. Dr. Martin Luther King, Jr., is arrested April 12 during a desegregation drive. By May 2, thousands have been arrested. On May 10, Attorney General Robert F. Kennedy calls for a halt to police action in Birmingham.

The violence and brutality of the Birmingham police shock the nation. Accounts of children being attacked by police dogs are a national disgrace. While these images win many whites over to the cause of civil rights, the police violence also convinces many blacks that Dr. King's nonviolent approach does not work. Many call for a more militant notion of black pride and black power. The fiery oratory of Muslim minister Malcolm X best articulates the rising black rage.

MALCOLM X ON BIRMINGHAM AND THE CIVIL RIGHTS MOVEMENT

President Kennedy did not send troops to Alabama when dogs were biting black babies. He waited three weeks until the situation exploded. He then sent troops after the Negroes had demonstrated the ability to defend themselves.... As Muslims we have analyzed all such [civil rights] legislation and found that none has solved the racial problem, from the Emancipation Proclamation to the [1954] Supreme Court decision. It was all hypocrisy. Nothing was solved.

May 17: The Senate passes a bill requiring equal pay for equal work regardless of gender. The bill is signed into law on June 10.

June 11: With Governor George C. Wallace blocking the doorway, the University of Alabama is forcibly integrated by federalized National Guard troops. Wallace had challenged both the White House and the civil rights movement: *I draw the line in the dust and toss the gauntlet before the feet of tyranny and I say segregation now, segregation tomorrow, segregation forever.*

June 12: Civil rights leader Medgar Evers is assassinated by a sniper in Jackson, Mississippi. President Kennedy joins the national outcry, as Evers is buried in Arlington National Cemetery.

July 1: The United Brotherhood of Carpenters, the largest building trade union, calls for its locals to end segregation.

August 28: Over 200,000 marchers descend on Washington, D.C., for the largest civil rights demonstration ever.

Dr. King delivers his "I Have a Dream" address, which galvanizes the movement and the nation.

FROM DR. MARTIN LUTHER KING, JR.'S, SPEECH, WASHINGTON, D.C.

I say to you today, my friends, that in spite of the difficulties and frustrations of the moment I still have a dream. It is a dream deeply rooted in the American dream.

I have a dream that one day this nation will rise up and live out the true meaning of its creed: "We hold these truths to be self-evident; that all men are created equal."

I have a dream that one day on the red hills of Georgia the sons of former slaves and the sons of former slaveowners will be able to sit down together at the table of brotherhood.

I have a dream that one day even the state of Mississippi, a desert state sweltering with the heat of injustice and oppression, will be transformed into an oasis of freedom and justice.

I have a dream that my four little children will one day live in a nation where they will not be judged by the color of their skin but by the content of their character.

I have a dream today.

I have a dream that one day the state of Alabama, whose governor's lips are presently dripping with the words of interposition and nullification, will be transformed into a situation where little black boys and girls will be able to join hands with little white boys and white girls and walk together as sisters and brothers.

I have a dream today.

I have a dream that one day every valley shall be exalted, every hill and mountain shall be made low, the rough places will be made plains, and the crooked places will be made straight, and the glory of the Lord shall be revealed, and all flesh shall see it together.

September 10: President Kennedy orders the National Guard to keep the public school system open in Huntsville, Alabama, after George Wallace had closed it.

September 15: Four young black girls are killed in a bomb explosion in a Birmingham, Alabama, church.

October 11: A U.S. government report, *American Women*, reports that the federal government should address discrimination against women in the areas of jury rights and personal property rights.

October 27: 225,000 students boycott classes in Chicago to protest segregated schools.

November 22: President John F. Kennedy is assassinated in Dallas, Texas.

1964

A West Coast gay organization, the Society for Individual Rights (SIR), is formed.

* * *

Franklin Kameny, the founder of the Mattachine Society of Washington, D.C., delivers a speech in New York City, calling for gay pride.

January 23: The 24th Amendment becomes law.

THE 24TH AMENDMENT

1. The right of citizens of the United States to vote in any primary or other election for President or Vice President, for electors for President or Vice President, or for Senator or Representative in Congress, shall not be denied or abridged by the United States or any State by reason of failure to pay any poll tax or other tax.

2. The Congress shall have power to enforce this article by appropriate legislation.

January 27: Senator Margaret Chase Smith (R-Maine) enters the race for the Republican presidential nomination.

May 25: The Supreme Court bans the practice of closing local schools to avoid desegregation.

June 10: The Senate ends a 75-day filibuster on the Civil Rights Act.

July 2: President Johnson signs the Civil Rights Act of 1964 into law.

From the Civil Rights Act of 1964

Sec. 201. (a) All persons shall be entitled to the full and equal enjoyment of the goods, services, facilities, privileges, advantages, and accommodations of any place of public accommodation, as defined in this section, without discrimination or segregation on the ground of race, color, religion, or national origin.

Designed primarily to end racial discrimination in employment, Title VII of the 1964 Civil Rights Act becomes a crucial element in the battle to end sexual discrimination. The word *sex* is added to its text only at the last moment by Representative Howard W. Smith, a staunch segregationist, who feels that this addition will make the bill unpalatable to the nearly all-male House. His tactic backfires, and discrimination against women becomes a federal offense.

August 4: Three civil rights workers—James Chaney, Andrew Goodman, and Michael Schwerner—are found murdered in Philadelphia, Mississippi.

October 14: Dr. Martin Luther King, Jr., is awarded the Nobel Peace Prize.

December 4: 21 men, many Klan members, are arrested for conspiring to kill Chaney, Goodman, and Schwerner.

Gay rights organizations, including the Mattachine Society and the Daughters of Bilitis, picket the White House, Pentagon, and Philadelphia's Independence Hall, calling for homosexual rights.

February 21: Malcolm X is assassinated in New York City.

March 7–11: Civil rights marchers in Selma, Alabama, are attacked by 200 state troopers. Unitarian minister James Reeb is beaten to death, and three whites are charged but found not guilty on December 10. President Johnson meets with Governor George Wallace and demands that brutality stop.

March 15: President Johnson submits voting rights legislation to Congress. He delivers what is perhaps the most forceful argument for civil rights ever articulated by an American president.

FROM PRESIDENT LYNDON JOHNSON'S INTRODUCTION
OF THE VOTING RIGHTS ACT

At times, history and fate meet at a single time in a single place to shape a turning point in a man's unending search for freedom.

So it was at Lexington and Concord. So it was a

century ago at Appomattox. So it was last week in Selma, Alabama.

There, long suffering men and women peacefully protested the denial of their rights as Americans. Many were brutally assaulted. One good man—a man of God—was killed. . . .

Our mission is at once the oldest and the most basic of this country—to right wrong, to do justice, to serve man. . . .

There is no Negro problem. There is no Southern problem. There is no Northern problem. There is only an American problem.

And we are met here tonight as Americans—not as Democrats or Republicans; we're met here as Americans to solve that problem.

This was the first nation in the history of the world to be founded with a purpose. The great phrases of that purpose still sound in every American heart, North and South:

"All men are created equal." "Government by consent of the governed." "Give me liberty or give me death."

And those are not just clever words, and those are not just empty theories.

In their name Americans have fought and died for two centuries and tonight around the world they stand there as guardians of our liberty risking their lives.

Those words are promised to every citizen that he shall share in the dignity of man. This dignity cannot be found in a man's possessions. It cannot be found in his power or in his position. It really rests on his right to be treated as a man equal in opportunity to all others. . . .

The history of this country in large measure is the history of expansion of that right to all of our people. Many of the issues of civil rights are very complex and most difficult. But about this there can and should be no argument: every American citizen must have an equal right to vote. . . .

Wednesday, I will send to Congress a law designed to eliminate illegal barriers to the right to vote. . . .

This bill will strike down restrictions to voting in all elections, federal, state and local, which have been used to deny Negroes the right to vote.

This bill will establish a simple, uniform standard which cannot be used, however ingenious the effort, to flout our Constitution. It will provide for citizens to be registered by officials of the United States Government, if the state officials refuse to register them.

It will eliminate tedious, unnecessary lawsuits which delay the right to vote.

Finally, this legislation will insure that properly registered individuals are not prohibited from voting. . . .

There is no constitutional issue here. The command of the Constitution is plain. There is no moral issue. It is wrong—deadly wrong—to deny any of your fellow Americans the right to vote in this country.

There is no issue of states' rights, or national rights. There is only the struggle for human rights. . . .

But even if we pass this bill the battle will not be over.

What happened in Selma is part of a far larger move-
ment which reaches into every section and state of
America. It is the effort of American Negroes to secure
for themselves the full blessings of American life.

Their cause must be our cause too. Because it's not just
Negroes, but really it's all of us who must overcome the
crippling legacy of bigotry and injustice. And we shall
overcome. . . .

March 17–21: A federal court rules that the Selma march
can proceed. On March 21, LBJ sends federal troops to
protect the Selma marchers. Leading 3,200 marchers,
Martin Luther King, Jr., begins a civil rights march from
Selma to Montgomery, Alabama.

March 25: Viola Gregg Liuzzo, a civil rights worker
from Detroit, is shot to death in Selma, Alabama. Three
Ku Klux Klan members are later found guilty and sentenced to 10 years in prison.

March 26: President Johnson declares war on the Ku
Klux Klan, calling it *a hooded society of bigots.*

April 1: Martin Luther King, Jr., proposes an economic
boycott of Alabama.

July 2: Title VII of 1964 Civil Rights Act goes into effect.

June 10–15: 350 people are arrested during mass demonstrations protesting the slow pace of school desegregation in Chicago.

* * *

July 13: Thurgood Marshall is nominated to be solicitor general of the United States.

August 6: President Johnson signs the Voting Rights Act of 1965.

August 11–16: Rising black frustration with racism, poverty, and police brutality sparks riots in the Watts section of Los Angeles, leaving 35 dead and $200 million in damage. LBJ assails the Watts rioters, likening them to Klansmen.

October 19: The House Un-American Activities Committee opens an investigation of the Ku Klux Klan.

1966

At Third National Conference of Governors' Commission on the Status of Women, 28 attendees break off to form the National Organization of Women (NOW).

From NOW's Statement of Purpose

We will protest and endeavor to change the false image of women now prevalent in the mass media and in the texts, ceremonies, laws and practices of our major social institutions ... church, state, college, factory or office which in the guise of protectiveness ... foster in women self-denigration, dependence and evasion of responsibil-

ity, undermine their confidence in their own abilities and foster contempt for women.

The Mattachine Society successfully challenges a New York State law that outlaws bars frequented by three or more known homosexuals.

February 7: An Alabama federal court rules that state laws barring women from jury duty *deny women equal protection of the laws in violation of the 14th Amendment.*

March 7: The Voting Rights Act of 1965 is upheld by the Supreme Court.

March 25: The Supreme Court declares all poll taxes to be an unconstitutional economic barrier to voting.

June 6: James Meredith is shot while on a lone voting registration march from Memphis, Tennessee, to Jackson, Mississippi. Representatives from 26 civil rights groups, including CORE, SNCC, NAACP and the SCLC complete the march. Along the way, many marchers are harassed, tear-gassed and arrested. A split also develops between the followers of King's philosophy of nonviolence and the growing militancy of black power advocates. Stokely Carmichael, Director of SNCC, is beaten and arrested on the march. Upon his release, he declares: *Never again will I take a beating without hitting back!*

* * *

August 5: During a civil rights march in Chicago, Martin Luther King, Jr., and other leading civil rights leaders are stoned by white residents.

September 22: After Dr. King publicly denounces the militancy of the black power movement, Stokely Carmichael publishes his definition of the movement in *The New York Review of Books*.

STOKELY CARMICHAEL ON BLACK POWER

Politically, black power means what it has always meant to SNCC: the coming-together of black people to elect representatives and to force those representatives to speak to their needs. It does not mean merely putting black faces into office. A man or a woman who is black and from the slums cannot be automatically expected to speak to the needs of black people. Most of the black politicians we see around the country today are not what SNCC means by black power. The power must be that of a community, and emanate from there.

October: Espousing a militant philosophy of black pride and separatism, the Black Panther party is founded in Oakland, California.

1967

In a policy reversal, the American Civil Liberties Union calls for an end to laws against homosexuality.

* * *

February 15: President Johnson exhorts Congress to pass his legislation ending discrimination in housing and jury selection.

April 15: At a rally of 100,000 in New York, Martin Luther King, Jr., joins forces with the antiwar movement.

June 10: Avowed racist Lester Maddox is sworn in as Georgia's governor.

June 12: The Supreme Court strikes down all state laws banning interracial marriage.

June 13: Thurgood Marshall, the great-grandson of a slave, is the first black American nominated to serve on the Supreme Court.

July 12–17: Black riots in Newark, New Jersey, leave 26 dead.

July 23–28: 43 people are killed as black riots engulf Detroit, Michigan.

August 17: Speaking from Cuba, black power activist Stokely Carmichael calls on American blacks to engage in "total revolution."

* * *

October 2: Thurgood Marshall is sworn in as Supreme Court justice.

November 7: Carl B. Stokes is elected mayor of Cleveland, the first black man to lead a major U.S. city.

1968

February 8: Segregationist George C. Wallace announces his candidacy for president on a law-and-order ticket.

February 29: The President's National Advisory on Civil Disorders (the Kerner Commission) condemns racism and calls for financial aid to black communities to avoid further racial polarization.

March 11: The Senate passes the Civil Rights Bill of 1968. LBJ praises the *nation's commitment to civil rights under law*.

April 4: Martin Luther King, Jr., is assassinated in Memphis. Riots ensue in Washington, D.C., and in 100 other American cities. King's funeral in Atlanta draws 75,000 mourners.

Reacting to the murder of Martin Luther King, Jr., President Johnson states that *Martin Luther King stands with our other American martyrs in the cause of freedom and justice*. Edward Brooke (R–Mass.), the first elected black senator since Reconstruction, declares: *In our an-*

guish and bitterness of this awful event, we must not lose sight of the meaning of this great man's life. The vindication of Dr. King's historic endeavors can only come through our renewed dedication to the human goals of brotherly love and equal justice which he so nobly advanced.

April 11: President Johnson signs the Civil Rights Act of 1968, outlawing discrimination in housing.

May 2: Ralph Abernathy leads thousands on a Poor People's March on Washington, D.C., where they establish a settlement of shanties and tents known as Resurrection City. The march had been planned by Dr. King to bring attention to the lasting problem of poverty in America.

June 6: Robert Kennedy dies in Los Angeles hours after being shot by an assassin.

June 8: James Earl Ray is arrested in London and charged with the murder of Martin Luther King.

June 24: The District of Columbia police clear Resurrection City and arrest 124 protesters.

December 1: The Women's Equity Action League (WEAL) is founded in Cleveland.

1969

January 3: Shirley Chisholm, an outspoken advocate of civil rights and women's liberation, takes her seat as the first black woman in the House of Representatives.

SHIRLEY CHISHOLM ON WOMEN'S LIBERATION

The law cannot do it for us. We must do it for ourselves. Women in this country must become revolutionaries. We must refuse to accept the traditional roles and stereotypes.... We must replace the old, negative thoughts about our femininity with positive thoughts and positive action.

March 16: James Earl Ray is sentenced to 99 years for the murder of Martin Luther King, Jr.

June 6: The FBI admits extensive wiretapping of Martin Luther King's telephones.

June 27–29: When New York City police attempt to raid the Stonewall Inn, a bar, gay patrons put up unexpected resistance. The ensuing riot becomes known as the "Stonewall Rebellion," a pivotal event leading to the rise of a highly politicized and organized movement, inspired by both the civil rights and antiwar efforts, demanding an end to discrimination and harassment, and instilling a sense of gay pride.

* * *

September 23: Secretary of Labor George Schulz orders compliance with the Philadelphia Plan guidelines, requiring labor unions working on buildings receiving federal funds to hire minority construction workers.

November: The Gay Activists Alliance (GAA) is formed. The GAA gains notoriety for its highly publicized demonstrations known as "zaps" against institutions engaging in discrimination and media that spread negative depictions of gay people.

December 4: Chicago police kill Black Panther leader Fred Hampton and a fellow Panther in a hail of unanswered gunfire.

1970

New York is the first city to ban sexual discrimination in public accommodations. The law is passed after women "liberate" the hitherto male-only bar of the Biltmore Hotel.

The first female Lutheran pastor is ordained.

The New York City Assembly holds hearings on a gay rights bill, the first legislative body ever to consider such action.

* * *

January 14: A federal court orders the Internal Revenue Service to end tax-exempt status for segregated private schools.

February 5–9: Southern senators John Stennis and Strom Thurmond demand that equal vigilance be applied to desegregating Northern school systems.

February 28: In controversial statement leaked to the press, presidential advisor Daniel Patrick Moynihan calls for a period of "benign neglect" with regard to federal efforts on civil rights.

March 24: In his civil rights address, President Nixon supports the principles of the *Brown* decision, but questions the wisdom of busing efforts to end school segregation.

May 6: Senator Birch Bayh (D–Ind.) opens hearings on the ERA.

August 26: Women's groups call a women's 24-hour general strike to commemorate the fiftieth anniversary of the 19th Amendment.

Publication of *Sisterhood Is Powerful*, an anthology of feminist essays, edited by Robin Morgan, captures the essence of the movement.

THE WOMEN'S LIBERATION MOVEMENT FROM *SISTERHOOD IS POWERFUL*, EDITED BY ROBIN MORGAN

This is not a movement one "joins." There are no rigid structures or membership cards. The Women's Liberation Movement exists where three or four friends or neighbors decide to meet regularly over coffee and talk about their personal lives. . . . It exists in your mind and in the political and personal insights that you can contribute to change and shape and help its growth.

1971

In Albany, New York, the first statewide gay rights demonstration draws 3,500 marchers.

The Professional Women's Caucus files a sex discrimination class-action suit against every all-male law school receiving federal funds.

January 25: In *Phillips v. Martin Marietta*, the first major sex discrimination decision based on the 1964 Civil Rights Act, the Supreme Court rules that business cannot deny employment to women with preschool children.

March 8: Files detailing extensive FBI surveillance and harassment of civil rights and antiwar activists are leaked to the news media.

* * *

April 8: Heavyweight champion Joe Frazier is the first black man since Reconstruction to address the South Carolina legislature.

April 14: The Supreme Court upholds the legality of busing to achieve school integration.

May 4: Repudiating segregation, Georgia Governor Jimmy Carter suggests that the "New South" has a healthier racial climate than the North.

May 17: Washington State passes the nation's first law against sexual discrimination in hiring and promotion.

June 15: In a 5-4 vote, the Supreme Court rules that communities can close public facilities rather than integrate them. Jackson, Mississippi, closes its public swimming pool.

June 17: The Air Force's Jeanne M. Holm becomes the nation's first woman brigadier general.

June 30: The 26th Amendment goes into effect, lowering the voting age to 18.

September 26: Shirley Chisholm enters the race for the Democratic presidential nomination. The nomination, she insists, is too important to be decided *entirely by white men.*

* * *

December 1: The Equal Employment Opportunity Commission charges AT&T with job discrimination against women, blacks, and Hispanics, and calls the company *the biggest oppressor of women in the United States.*

1972

January: The first issue of *Ms.* magazine appears on newsstands.

March 22: The Senate passes the Equal Rights Amendment and sends it to the states for ratification.

THE EQUAL RIGHTS AMENDMENT

1. Equality of rights under the law shall not be denied or abridged by the United States or by any State on account of sex.

2. The Congress shall have the power to enforce, by appropriate legislation, the provisions of this article.

3. This amendment shall take effect two years after the date of ratification.

May 18: Magie Kuhn, 67, founds the Gray Panther party to fight discrimination against the elderly.

MAGIE KUHN ON THE RIGHTS AND
DUTIES OF THE ELDERLY

Arbitrary retirement is a social waste.... Men and women approaching retirement should be recycled for public service work, and their companies should foot the bill. We can no longer afford to scrap-pile people.

July 14: At the Democratic National Convention, 40% of the delegates are women. Jean Westwood is chosen to chair the party's National Committee, the first woman to do so. Jim Foster, an openly gay delegate, addresses the convention.

July 7: Susan Lynn and Joanne E. Pierce are sworn in as the nation's first female FBI agents.

October 12–13: Senate liberals filibuster to block anti-busing legislation.

November 8: 500 Native Americans end a sit-in at the Bureau of Indian Affairs, when the bureau agrees to consider their complaints about treaty violations and exploitation of natural resources on reservations.

December 9: "I am Woman," a popular song of women's liberation, reaches number one on *Billboard*'s charts.

1973

January 18: AT&T agrees to pay $15 million in damages to women and minority victims of discrimination.

* * *

January 22: In *Roe v. Wade*, the Supreme Court strikes down state laws restricting a woman's right to abortion, arguing that the right to privacy is *broad enough to encompass a woman's decision whether or not to terminate her pregnancy.*

FROM JUSTICE HARRY A. BLACKMUN'S DECISION IN
ROE ET AL. V. WADE

We therefore conclude that the right of personal privacy includes the abortion decision, but that this right is not unqualified and must be considered against important state interests in regulation. . . .

January 22: Dr. Alan F. Guttmacher, president of the Planned Parenthood Federation of America, calls the *Roe* decision *a wise and courageous stroke for the right to privacy, and for the protection of women's physical and emotional health. . . . Hundreds of thousands of women every year will be spared the medical risks and emotional horrors of back-street and self-induced abortions.*

February 22: President Nixon affirms his support of the ERA.

February 27: The militant American Indian Movement (AIM) stages an armed occupation of Wounded Knee, South Dakota, the site of an Indian massacre in 1890.

* * *

October 16: Maynard Jackson is elected mayor of Atlanta, the first black mayor of a major Southern city.

November: The National Gay Task Force is formed in New York City, with Jean O'Leary and Bruce Voeller as co-directors. The group aspires to *re-educate society ... to esteem gay men and women at their full human worth and to accord them places in society which will allow them to attain and contribute according to their full human and social potential.*

November 7: The New Jersey Supreme Court rules that the Hoboken Little League must open its ranks to girls.

December 15: Reversing a 100-year-old opinion, the American Psychiatric Association declares that homosexuality is not a mental illness.

December 17: The Federal Home Loan Bank Board orders an end to discrimination against women in granting mortgages.

1974

Bank America denies Kathryn Kirschbaum a credit card without the signature of her husband, despite the fact that she is mayor of Davenport, Iowa.

* * *

In *Milliken v. Bradley*, a case involving Detroit and its suburbs, the Supreme Court votes 5-4 against ordering desegregation across district lines. In his dissent, Justice Thurgood Marshall argues that the case has more to do with the turn of popular opinion against busing than with justice.

FROM THURGOOD MARSHALL DISSENT IN MILLIKEN V. BRADLEY

Desegregation is not and was not ever expected to be an easy task. Racial attitudes ingrained in our nation's childhood and adolescence are not easily thrown aside in its middle years. But just as the convictions of some cannot be allowed to stand in the way of the rights of others, so public opposition, no matter how strident, cannot be permitted to divert this court from the enforcement of the constitutional principles in this case.

Today's holding, I fear, is more a perceived reflection of a public mood that we have done far enough in insuring the Constitution's guarantee of equal justice than it is a product of neutral principles of law. In the short run, it may be the easier course to allow our great metropolitan areas to be divided up into two cities—one white, the other black—but it is a course, I predict, our people will ultimately regret.

I dissent.

* * *

June 12: Little League Baseball is opened to girls on a national level.

August 23: President Ford declares August 26 as Women's Equality Day and urges ratification of the ERA.

September 12: Violence erupts in Boston, as students and parents protest court-ordered busing.

October 29: President Ford signs a bill requiring the FDIC to end sexual discrimination when granting credit.

1975

The UN declares 1975 the International Women's Year.

January 21: In *Taylor v. Louisiana*, the Supreme Court bans automatic exclusion of women from jury duty.

March 11: The U.S. Civil Rights Commission reports that the percentage of black students in predominately white schools is higher in the South than in the North.

February 1: Otis Francis Tabler is the first admitted homosexual to receive security clearance from the Defense Department.

* * *

May 27: The National Academy of Science reports a drastic reduction in the number of abortion-related deaths since legalization.

June 3: The U.S. Department of Health, Education, and Welfare establishes guidelines affirming the right of female students to participate in school athletic competitions.

August 6: The Voting Rights Act of 1965 is extended for an additional seven years.

September 28: Congress passes a bill authorizing admission of women to all three military academies.

November 4: On a popular ballot, the Equal Rights Amendment is rejected by voters in New York and New Jersey.

1976

February 13: Anti-ERA activist Phyllis Schafly claims that the ERA will turn all child care over to the federal government.

July 12: Representative Barbara C. Jordan (D–Tex.) is the first black woman to deliver the keynote address at the Democratic National Convention.

* * *

November 2: Supported by both Southern whites and black voters, former Georgia governor Jimmy Carter is the first president elected from the Deep South since the Civil War.

1977

January 1: Jacqueline Means is ordained in Indianapolis as the first Episcopal woman priest.

March 20: A delegation of leaders from 24 homosexual rights movements is received by President Carter's aides at the White House.

April 28: The Department of Health, Education, and Welfare outlines a ban on all discrimination against the physically handicapped by employers or educational institutions receiving federal funding.

June 7: In a campaign marked by the emotional appeals of singer Anita Bryant, conservatives, and fundamentalist churches, voters in Dade County, Florida, vote 2-1 to repeal a civil rights law protecting homosexuals against discrimination in employment, housing and public accommodations. The campaign galvanizes gay political activity nationwide. Miami gay activist John W. Campbell sees the voting as the beginning of a stronger movement: *For decades homosexuality was the love that dare not speak its name. Now the whole world is talking about our cause. We are everywhere. We are not going to go away. And we are going to win.*

November 18–21: The First National Women's Conference in Houston, the largest feminist council since Seneca Falls, draws 1,442 delegates and calls for passage of the ERA.

November: Harvey Milk, an openly gay politician, is the first homosexual elected to the San Francisco Board of Supervisors.

1978

The Civil Service Reform Act bars discrimination against gays in civilian government positions.

April–May: The cities of St. Paul, Minnesota, Eugene, Oregon, and Wichita, Kansas, vote to repeal their gay rights laws.

May 11: Margaret A. Brewer becomes the first woman Marine Corps general.

June: 250,000 people in San Francisco rally for gay rights and to protest the proposed Briggs amendment, which will expel from California's schools all gays, lesbians, or heterosexuals speaking favorably of homosexuality.

* * *

June 28: In *Bakke v. Regents of University of California*, the Supreme Court rules that Alan Bakke, a white student, was discriminated against because of racial quotas favoring black students.

July 9: 100,000 men and women demonstrate in favor of the ERA, with three states short of ratification.

October 6: Congress extends the deadline for ERA ratification to June 30, 1982.

October 10: Congress authorizes the minting of a Susan B. Anthony dollar coin.

November: Californians defeat the Briggs amendment; Seattle votes overwhelmingly to retain its gay rights laws.

November 27: San Francisco Mayor George Moscone and City Supervisor Harvey Milk are assassinated by Dan White, a disgruntled former city supervisor. As perhaps the most publicly gay politician in America, Milk knew that he had many enemies. He had left a note with a friend to be released in the event of his assassination. In this note he calls on supporters of gay rights to channel their anger into constructive action.

FROM HARVEY MILK'S NOTE TO BE READ IN THE EVENT OF HIS ASSASSINATION

I cannot prevent anybody from getting angry or mad or frustrated [at my assassination]. I can only hope that they'll turn that anger and frustration and madness into something positive so that hundreds will step forward, so that gay doctors come out, the gay lawyers, gay judges, gay bankers, gay architects. I hope that every professional gay would just say "enough!" come forward and tell everybody, wear a sign, let the world know. Maybe that will help. These are my strong requests, knowing that it could happen, hoping that it doesn't ... and if it does, I think I've already achieved something. I think it's been worth it.

1979

February 13: The U.S. Civil Rights Commission states that 46% of American students still attend segregated schools, 25 years after the *Brown v. Board of Education* decision.

February 3: Jane M. Byrne is elected the first woman mayor of Chicago.

June 27: The Supreme Court gives qualified endorsement of private affirmative action programs.

October 14: The first National March on Washington for Gay and Lesbian Rights draws more than 100,000 participants.

1980

___

February 8: President Carter issues a military selective service plan that calls for drafting women.

April 11: The Equal Employment Opportunity Commission releases regulations prohibiting sexual harassment of women by their male superiors.

May 28: First women graduate from the military academies.

July: 75 openly gay delegates attend the Democratic National Convention. Melvin Boozer, president of the Washington Chapter of the Gay Activist Alliance, is symbolically nominated for vice-president, and addresses the convention before a national television audience. The party platform includes a clause stating: *All groups must be protected from discrimination based on race, color, religion, national origin, language, age, sex, or sexual orientation.*

July 15: For the first time in decades, the Republican National Convention does not endorse the Equal Rights Amendment.

1981

___

February 23: A federal court in Detroit rules that schools are not obligated to provide equal athletic programs for male and female students.

* * *

April 4: City Councilman Henry Gabriel Cisneros is elected mayor of San Antonio, Texas, the first Spanish-surnamed mayor of a major U.S. city.

April 23: At Senate hearings on abortion rights, six women are arrested after chanting: *Not the church, not the state, women must decide their fate.*

June 16: President Reagan asks his attorney general to determine whether the nation is still well served by the Voting Rights Act of 1965.

July 7: President Reagan nominates Sandra Day O'Connor to the Supreme Court, the first woman to serve on the Court.

1982

January 2: Reagan declares opposition to "rigid quotas" in hiring and promotion of women and minorities.

Wisconsin is the first state to pass a gay rights law.

February 25: The Reagan administration asks the Supreme Court to decide the constitutionality of tax-exempt status for all-white private schools.

June 23: Congress extends the Voting Rights Act of 1965.

* * *

June 7: As chance of ratification slips away, thousands demonstrate in Chicago in favor of the ERA, including Mayor Jane Byrne and former first lady Betty Ford.

June 30: The deadline for passing the Equal Rights Amendment passes after failure to secure ratification by 38 states.

1983

April 12: Representative Harold Washington is elected as the first black mayor of Chicago, symbolizing black urban power.

May 25: The Supreme Court votes 8-1 against tax exemptions for segregated schools.

June 15: In five related decisions, the Supreme Court narrowly upholds *Roe v. Wade*'s constitutional protection of abortion rights.

June 28: The Senate votes 50-49 in favor of an abortion amendment that allows state legislatures to limit or abolish the right to abortion. The vote falls short of the two-thirds majority needed to send it to the states for ratification.

June 18–24: Teacher Sally K. Ride becomes the first U.S. woman in space on the second voyage of the space shuttle *Challenger*.

* * *

August 30–September 5: Air Force Lt. Col. Guion S. Bluford, Jr., becomes the first U.S. black astronaut in space, aboard space shuttle *Challenger*.

October 20: The Senate votes 78-23 to establish a national holiday to observe Martin Luther King, Jr.'s, birthday on the third Monday of January. North Carolina Senator Jesse Helms attacks King's "Marxism."

November 4: Civil rights leader Jesse Jackson announces his candidacy for president.

1984

January 5: President Reagan appoints Linda Chavez to head the U.S. Civil Rights Commission. She urges study of the "radical principle" of equal pay for equal work.

July 1: NOW passes a resolution calling for nomination of a woman for vice-president in 1984.

July 16–19: The Democratic party nominates Geraldine Ferraro for vice-president, the first woman nominated for national office by a major party.

During Jesse Jackson's unsuccessful campaign for the Democratic nomination, hundreds of thousands of new voters are registered, many of them urban and Southern blacks who have never before participated in politics. At the Democratic National Convention, Jackson delivers a moving speech explaining what it is like to be poor and alienated from the American Dream.

FROM JESSE JACKSON'S ADDRESS TO THE 1984 DEMOCRATIC CONVENTION

Most poor people are not on welfare. . . .

I know they work. I'm a witness. They catch the early bus. They work every day. They raise other people's children. They work every day. They clean the streets. They work every day. They drive vans with cabs. They work every day. They change the beds you slept in these hotels last night and can't get a union contract. They work every day. . . .

They work in hospitals. I know they do. They wipe the bodies of those who are sick with fever and pain. They empty their bedpans. They clean out their commode. No job is beneath them, and yet when they get sick, they cannot lie in the bed they made up every day. America, that is not right. We are a better nation than that. . . .

October 11: In a spirited debate, Geraldine Ferraro accuses Vice-President Bush of being "patronizing" toward her.

1985

January 22: President Reagan addresses the March for Life anti-abortion rally in Washington, D.C.

* * *

March 26: The Supreme Court reverses an Oklahoma decision that permitted a teacher to be fired for speaking in public about gay rights.

May 12: Amy Eilberg is ordained as the first woman Conservative rabbi.

October 23: Two Supreme Court Justices criticize Attorney General Edwin Meese's suggestion that the Court base decisions on the "original intent of the founding fathers." Justice Paul Stevens says this notion ignores the importance of amendments passed after the Civil War, particularly the 14th Amendment. Justice William Brennan characterizes Meese's suggestion as *little more than arrogance cloaked in humility.*

* * *

November 19: Representative Patricia Schroeder (D–Colo.) attacks Presidential advisor Donald T. Regan for stating that arms control talks are *too complicated for women to understand.*

1986

January 20: First official observation of the Martin Luther King holiday.

March 9: 125,000 people demonstrate in Washington in favor of abortion rights.

* * *

April 17: Jesse Jackson forms the National Rainbow Coalition to promote liberal and progressive views within the Democratic party.

June 5: The Senate Judiciary Committee rejects Jefferson B. Sessions, a Reagan nominee for a federal judgeship, because of his insensitivity to civil rights and his cavalier remarks about the Ku Klux Klan.

June 17: Donald Regan remarks that anti-apartheid sanctions against South Africa would be *asking the women of America to give up their jewelry.*

June 19: In *Meritor Savings Bank v. Vinson*, the Supreme Court rules that sexual harassment of an employee violates federal law.

July 11: In a narrow decision, the Supreme Court reaffirms constitutional protection of abortion rights.

June 30: The Supreme Court rules that homosexual relations, even in private between consenting adults, are not protected by the Constitution. The decision upholds a Georgia anti-sodomy law from 1816.

September 17: Despite opposition by civil rights and women's organizations, the Senate confirms William H. Rehnquist as chief justice by a vote of 65-33.

1987

Representative Barney Frank (D–Mass.) publicly admits his homosexuality. He is later reelected with a large majority of the vote.

The U.S. Court of Appeals orders the Army to reinstate Miriam ben-Shalom, who had been discharged after admitting her lesbianism.

January 24: 10,000 marchers demonstrate in Cummings, a town in Forsythe County, Georgia, that has remained all-white since 1912. Marchers include Atlanta Mayor Andrew Young, Coretta Scott King, Senator Sam Nunn, and Jesse Jackson.

July 1: President Reagan announces his nomination of Appeals Court Judge Robert H. Bork to fill the Supreme Court seat vacated by Louis Powell. Noted for his conservative views, including the opinion that there is no constitutional right to privacy, Bork's nomination is quickly opposed by the NAACP, NOW, and the National Education Association (NEA).

October 6: In a 9-5 vote the Senate Judiciary Committee fails to recommend Bork's nomination.

October 11: In Washington, D.C., more than 200,000 gay rights activists call for an end to discrimination based on sexual preference and for increased federal funding for AIDS research. On October 13 over 600 activists are arrested on the steps of the Supreme Court Building while protesting the court's 1986 ruling upholding a Georgia sodomy law.

October 23: The Senate rejects the Bork nomination by a vote of 58-42. The following month, Reagan nominates Appeals Court Judge Anthony M. Kennedy, a conservative.

1988

February 5: A movement to recall Arizona governor Evan Mecham for his refusal to observe the Martin Luther King holiday gathers momentum. He is removed from office April 5.

March 22: Congress overrides President Reagan's veto of the Civil Rights Restoration Act, which provides greater federal powers to prevent discrimination in institutions receiving federal aid.

April 25: The Supreme Court, in *Wards's Cove Packing Co. v. Antonio*, rules in a 5-4 vote that the burden of proof in discrimination cases rests with the plaintiff. This reverses an earlier ruling used as the basis for most anti-discrimination suits.

* * *

November 8: After a campaign noted for its emotional appeals to racial fears and patriotism, George Bush is elected 41st president.

1989

February 10: Ronald H. Brown, a black attorney, is named chairman of the Democratic party, the first black man to lead a major political party.

July 3: In *Webster v. Reproductive Health Services*, the Supreme Court votes 5-4 to uphold a Missouri law restricting abortion rights. Justice Harry Blackmun, the author of the *Roe v. Wade* decision, comments: *I fear for the future . . . the signs are evident and very obvious, and a chill wind blows.*

August 10: Army General Colin L. Powell is nominated to serve as Chairman of the Joint Chiefs of Staff. Powell is the first black and the youngest man to assume this position.

November 7: Douglas Wilder is elected governor of Virginia, the first black governor since Reconstruction.

November 18: The Pennsylvania legislature passes a law restricting abortion. Most abortions at public hospitals are banned. For all abortions, prior notification of spouse and a 24-hour waiting period is required.

1990

February 13: The American Bar Association votes overwhelmingly to support constitutional protection of abortion rights.

March 30: Idaho Governor Cecil Andrus vetoes a bill that would ban most abortions in the state.

April 23: President Bush signs the Hate Crime Statistics Act, requiring the federal government to keep records of crimes motivated by ethnic, religious, racial, or sexual prejudice.

April 28: Vice-President Dan Quayle addresses an anti-abortion rally in Washington, D.C., attended by 200,000.

July 7–26: Louisiana Governor Buddy Roemer vetoes two bills that would have outlawed all abortions except those to save the mother's life.

June 20–30: Nelson Mandela, deputy president of the African National Congress, tours the United States. Freed after 27 years in prison, Mandela is a living symbol of the struggle to end South Africa's policy of apartheid. While on his triumphant tour of America, Mandela thanks Americans for their support and reflects on America's contribution to change in South Africa.

From Nelson Mandela's Atlanta Address of June 27, 1990

Dr. King's dreams are now becoming the stuff of reality. At the time he began his anti-racist civil rights crusade there were only 300 elected black officials. Today it fills me with pride to know that there are nearly 6,000 black elected officials in this country. His dreams are suddenly going to see the light of day in our country as well.

July 13: Congress passes the Americans with Disabilities Act, requiring businesses to give equal access to disabled Americans.

July 20: Supreme Court Justice William Brennan announces his retirement; President Bush will appoint David Souter, adding another conservative vote to the Supreme Court.

October 6: David Duke, a former Klansman and neo-Nazi, receives 44% of the vote in his bid to be U.S. senator from Louisiana.

October 20: Citing his disapproval of quotas, President Bush vetoes the Civil Rights Act of 1990, which would allow victims of discrimination to collect for damages.

December 11: The assistant secretary of education Michael Williams condemns scholarships for minority students as discriminatory and in violation of civil rights laws.

December 18: Reversing his decision on minority scholarships, Michael Williams states that he was "politically naive" in announcing his previous policy.

1991

January–March: U.S. and allied military forces overwhelm Iraqi forces and liberate Kuwait. The short war marks the first time tens of thousands of women serve in a war zone. Women are also among the war's casualties. It is also notable that racially integrated U.S. forces score a smashing military victory. This is in distinct contrast to the racial tensions and violence during the Vietnam War.

March 3: A videocamera reveals several Los Angeles policemen in a brutal attack on a black man. The attack focuses nationwide attention on police brutality and racism.

June 5: In a 273-158 vote, the House passes a new version of the Civil Rights Bill.

June 27: Judge Thurgood Marshall announces his intention to resign.

* * *

July 1: President Bush nominates Clarence Thomas to succeed Thurgood Marshall on the Supreme Court. Thomas, a conservative black with little judicial experience, espouses black self-help and criticizes racial quotas. His nomination is quickly opposed by NOW, the NAACP, the NEA, and the AFL-CIO.

July–August: Operation Rescue, a militant anti-abortion group, stages a prolonged confrontation at a Wichita, Kansas, abortion clinic, resulting in hundreds of arrests. Federal troops are required to maintain order.

September 27: Deadlocked 7-7, the Senate Judiciary Committee sends the Clarence Thomas nomination to the full Senate for confirmation without any recommendation. During his testimony, Thomas offers few insights into his views on *Roe v. Wade*, the right to privacy, and other key issues.

October 15: After days of often lurid testimony regarding Clarence Thomas's alleged sexual harassment of subordinate Anita Hill, Thomas is confirmed by the Senate in a 52-48 vote.

November 2: Jesse Jackson announces that he will not be a candidate for president in 1992.

November 5: In the state of Washington voters narrowly pass a ballot initiative guaranteeing women the right to abortion even if the Supreme Court reverses *Roe v. Wade*.

November 21: Amid confusion and controversy, President Bush signs the Civil Rights Bill of 1991, after an aide had tried to impose a conservative interpretation that would reverse federal affirmative action regulations in place since 1965. Under fire from civil rights leaders and members of his own party, Bush signs the bill and declares: *This Administration is committed to action that is truly affirmative, positive action in every sense, to strike down all barriers to advancement of every kind for all people.*

BIBLIOGRAPHY

Adam, Barry D. *The Rise of a Gay and Lesbian Movement*, Boston, G.K. Hall, 1987.

Bell, Derrek. *Race, Racism and American Law*, Boston, Little Brown, 1973.

Blumenfeld, Warren J. and Raymond, Diane. *Looking at Gay and Lesbian Life*, Boston, Beacon Press, 1988.

Carruth, Gorton. *The Encyclopedia of American Facts & Dates*, Eighth Edition, New York, Harper & Row, 1987.

Carruth, Gorton and Ehrlich, Eugene. *The Harper Book of American Quotations*, New York, Harper & Row, 1988.

Du Bois, William Edward Burghardt. *The Emerging Thought of W.E.B. Du Bois: Essays and Editorials from the Crisis*, New York, Simon & Schuster, 1972.

Friedan, Betty. *The Feminist Mystique*, New York, Dell, 1963.

Hinton, Richard Josiah. *John Brown and His Men*, New York, Funk and Wagnalls, 1894.

Hoffman, Mark S., ed. *The World Almanac and Book of Facts*, New York, Pharos Books 1983–92.

Hymowitz, Carol and Weissman, Michaele. *A History of Women in America*, New York, Bantam, 1978.

King, Martin Luther. *Stride Toward Freedom*, New York, Harper & Row, 1958.

Low, W. Augustus and Clift, Virgil A. *Encyclopedia of Black America*, New York, Da Capo Press, 1984.

McKissack, Patricia and Frederick. *The Civil Rights Movement in America: From 1865 to the Present*, Chicago, Childrens Press, 1987.

Meltzer, Milton. ed. *The Black Americans: A History in their Own Words*, New York, Thomas Y. Crowell, 1984.

Morgan, Robin. ed. *Sisterhood is Powerful*, New York, Random House, 1970.

Ploski, Harry A. and Williams, James, eds. *The Negro Almanac: A Reference Work on the African American*, Fifth Edition, Detroit, Gale Research Press, 1989.

Ravitch, Diane. ed. *The American Reader: Words That Moved a Nation*, New York, Harper Collins, 1991.

Schlesinger, Arthur, M. Jr. gen. ed. *The Almanac of American History*, New York, Perigee Books, 1983.

Trager, James, ed. *The People's Chronology*, New York, Holt, Rinehart and Winston, 1979.

World Almanac, The Editors of. *The Little Red, White & Blue Book*, New York, Pharos Books, 1987.

Zinn, Howard. *A People's History of the United States*, New York, Harper Colophon, 1980.

INDEX